Terrorist Minds

by PK WU

ISBN-13: 978-1484942789
ISBN-10: 1484942787

Dedication

To all the dedicated and brave members of our armed forces, intelligence, law enforcement, and firefighting agencies who sacrifice their safety and lives on a daily basis to protect the American people from enemies, both foreign and domestic.

And to our nation's leaders, though often disagreeing and grid locked on particular policies and expenditures, always have our people's survival and prosperity at heart. May they show the wisdom that is necessary to defeat terrorists.

In memory of all the brave souls who have given their lives, bodies and minds in the service of America, American ideals and the American way of life. God bless America and Godspeed to all who fight the good fight against terrorism.

Forward

The ideas and letters to the CIA and FBI contained in this book were penned soon after the 911 terrorists attacks on the World Trade Center buildings in New York City. There was a swell of patriotism and support for our government's anti-terrorism policies and fighting a two front war in Iraq and Afghanistan.

The letters sent to our intelligence community were never acknowledged as received and there is no confirmation that either FBI or CIA officials were ever aware of my unsolicited correspondence, analyses, and suggestions. I'm certain they have more qualified professionals working on the complex problems of domestic and international terrorism whether state sponsored, jihad-inspired, lone wolves with grudges, al-Qaeda affiliates or whatever.

The intent of this book is to continue the dialog and awareness of the American public on the nature of terrorism and what each individual and their communities can do about it to safeguard their lives and property. No access to classified information from government sources was ever sought or granted and no government secrets are contained in this book, mostly written between 2002-2004.

Terrorist Minds

By PK WU

Table of Contents

Chapter One – The Mindset

Say the word "terrorist" and people will turn their heads in alarm. Their minds become filled with mental images of death, mayhem, bombings, and religious fanatics. Stereotypes of fanatical crazed killers strike fear into the hearts of peace loving people who have never experienced terror except in their imaginations based upon media news and action movies. But what of the child who fears walking through a neighborhood filled with wild dog packs, robbers, drug abusers, drunks, gangs, child molesters and killers? Do these children feel terrorized and anxious about surviving another walk to and from school and perhaps worry about their safety at school? What about the single female who lives in a dangerous area because that's all she can afford for herself and her children? Every stranger and late night footstep can portend a potential future event with possible bad endings for victims and all who feel vulnerable to troubled individuals with terrorist minds.

Let's consider a short list of more recent acts of terror:

1 The Boston Marathon bombings by self-styled jihadist brothers upset about involvement in Afghanistan and Iraq.

2 The Newtown Connecticut mass murders of 26 children and adults including the shooter's own mother.

3 The murders of our Ambassador to Lybia and three other Americans by al-Qaeda affiliates.

4 North Korea's leader repeatedly threatening to nuke the mainland, with provocative movement of missiles.

As our nation continues to grieve over the heinous murders our children due to gun violence, our nation's leaders are again mired in political infighting and deadlock. The Republicans have chosen once again to politicize every issue, even those that have no real political foundations. Obviously, they want President Obama and Democrats to fail at all cost to bolster their chances of winning seats during mid-term elections next year. Unfortunately, our innocent children have become disposable collateral to the GOP leadership due to their allegiance to the NRA. It is unlikely prominent GOP leaders will support rational gun control until their children fall victims to gun violence, and no one who loves America's potential future would wish that on anyone, not even on the sons of Satanic terrorists.

Those who use 2nd Amendment rights to argue for the widespread sale of assault weapons with large magazines need to read the Constitution that states only, "...the right of the people to keep and bear arms shall not be infringed." It doesn't say that requires the citizenry to possess any specific types of weapons, nor does it prohibit the government from regulating the nature of weaponry as there already exist laws against machine guns, grenades, rocket launchers, mortars and other weapons of mass destruction – except for high capacity assault weapons and semi automatic pistols.

Critics of reasonable gun control measures such as universal background checks complain that the issue of gun violence is too complex for legislative measures, therefore we should do nothing that do not address the causes of violence in our society. The root causes of violence are multi-faceted and includes genetic, environmental, cultural, social, socioeconomic, medical, and political reasons. Let's take a look at the primary cultural incentives to violent thought, speech and behavior in American society.

1. Glamorization of aggression and violence in movies, video games, and contact sports such as football and full contact fighting.
2. Sensationalistic and obsessive media blitz to provide violent news to viewers to boost or sustain television ratings that translate to higher advertising income.
3. Continued involvement of America in various wars throughout our children's' lifetimes as if legitimized killing is a normal part of life where the most proficient killers become our highest regarded heroes.
4. Gender role models and identification by boys and young men who become thrilled with hunting and killing innocent animals for sport.
5. Easy availability of weapons of mass murder with high ammo clips… assault weapons that if used for hunting would live little game trophies after the kills. Hunting sportsmanship requires one shot one sudden kill, not a barrage of bullets.
6. Undiagnosed, untreated, untreatable mental illness in emotionally unstable individuals who are prone to violent thoughts, with or without a prior record of arrests and treatment.
7. Schools do not teach individual real world responsibility and problem solving methods but instead primarily teach to the "3 Rs" academic test standards.

8. Certain individuals are genetically prone toward aggression and violence and as children are not taught how to deal with frustration, rage and hatred.
9. Other contributing causes that have high potential for violent behaviors.

Beware of *TYPE A - Terrorist* Personalities

Research into behavioral propensities for violence based on genetic factors that might affect brain chemistry and thought have not disclosed reliable physical causation for bullying, violent speech and action or terrorism. Instead, the predominant causes of violent behavior appear to be reaction to personal experiences, perception of reality, and environmental influences from people, ideas, media, entertainment and mental illness.

People with *Type A aggressive* personalities share many characteristics that distinguish them from most people. Those people who are *Type A* are also known as *Alpha males*, and are often referred to as "assholes" by workers who are abused by *Type A* bosses. Females with *Type A* personalities are often referred to as "aggressive bitches" that are arrogant, argumentative, dramatic, and highly demanding of others.

The personality expression of *Type A* people, especially males are:

1. Abrasive in attitude and speech, which tends to be critical and rude.
2. Abrupt and curt, showing little consideration of other people.
3. Absorbed with self interest, with no concern for others.

4. Addictive to money, risk-taking, power, possessions, and acclaim.

5. Aggressive toward competitors or people who are obstacles.

6. Angry when they don't get their way at the time they want it.

7. Antagonistic, critical, and insulting when threatened or competing.

8. Anti-authority because they hate being told what to do.

9. Autocratic as bosses, spouses, teachers, parents or acquaintances.

10. Antithetical; always seeking to criticize and discredit others.

11. Anti-social as being nice is equated with kissing ass, a weakness.

12. Argumentative when challenged, because they feel always right.

13. Arrogant attitude in believing their superiority, compared to others.

14. Assaulting and inciting when not getting their way when they want.

15. Audacious and ridiculously impatient and demanding.

16. Avarice is a motivating drive in obtaining money, power, and status.

17. Avenging losses by trying to destroy competitors, for satisfaction.

18. Absolute in their ideas, attitudes, and knowledge; closed-minded.

19. Ambitious to the max, wanting to be the boss, never the follower.

20. Acquiring worldly goods; money, property, prestige, and power.

21. Assumptive in worldview and perspectives as being correct.
22. Assured in ability to manipulate, control, persist, and win at all cost.
23. Atheistic because no one can be above them, not even God.
24. Arbitrary in decision-making and judgments, feeling always right.
25. Abusive when expectations are not fulfilled, and they get impatient.
26. Accustomed to being served by others, being on top and in control.
27. Aggrandizing their own importance to the deference of all others.
28. Accusatory of others, without seeking evidence or proof of errors.
29. Annoying everyone around them, who are forced to tolerate them.
30. Advancing their agendas and not leaving fate to others or chance.

Type A's use aggressive behavior to hide emotional insecurities as:

1. Aberrations such as mistreatment of animals and sex perversions.
2. Adultery due to need to feel in control and get what they want.
3. Addiction to try controlling what they can't; gambling, sex, and drugs.
4. Alcoholism is disguised as social drinking, a way to mask unhappiness.

5. Anal-retentive need to control others by holding back cooperation.
6. Anxieties due to fear of failing to meet expectations of self or others.
7. Apprehensions from childhood, which they overcompensate as adults.
8. Atrociousness or meanness due to spoiled, demanding behavior habits.
9. Authoritarian tendency due to familiarity and not subject to uncertainty.
10. Absence of talents, skills or abilities, which they expect from others.
11. Abuse by Type A parents, bullies or other adults during childhood.

Type A, Alpha personalities view themselves in a more positive light, as their mirrors reflect a distorted and self-deceptive view of their own narcissistic beauty and power.

1. Adamant because they feel they're right, and other people are wrong.
2. Attractive traits such as strength, determination, ambition, and status.
3. Accomplishment due to persistence and never giving up on self.
4. Affluence in greater accumulation of wealth, possessions and status.
5. Advantaged by birthright, genetics, class, and personal constitution.

6. Analytical of situations, rules, people, and data to plot beneficial path.
7. Assertive insistence on personal freedoms, rights, and entitlements.
8. Assured and confident of ability to succeed, win, and reach one's goals.
9. Autonomous and independent minded, not needing other opinions.
10. Atypical and unique, unlike the normal herds of followers and masses.
11. All knowing of what is crucial and germane to attainment of goals.
12. Aristocratic entitlement, as they are leaders and superior to others.
13. Adept at sizing up situations and people, then making their moves.
14. Able to mount a solid offense and strong defense in competition.
15. Astute in their fields of endeavor, as they strive to be one of the best.
16. Appealing to others due to natural leadership qualities and strengths.
17. Acclaim, admiration and accolades are deserved and expected.
18. Accurate perception of reality permits realistic manipulation and action.
19. Adventurous nature justifies risk taking to push the system to its max.

20. Adonis complex in viewing others relative to their personal promotion.

21. Almighty as bosses, leaders, judges and police due to power positions.

22. Ambitious pursuit of worldly goals; money, power, property, control.

23. Actuating others to perform at high level, where they might slack off.

24. Accumulating possession, status, power and wealth to validation self.

25. Adroit in changing situations around to their advantage and benefit.

26. Adjudicating the unknown, unpredictable, and uncertain by decisions.

27. Advantaged due to innate superiority as compared to others.

28. Asset conscious, accumulating, hoarding, building self-monuments.

Type A personalities expect others to be subordinate in their behavior:

1. Acceptance of their orders, directions, and rules without question.

2. Accommodating their whims, quirks, changes, demands and attitudes.

3. Acknowledgement of their superior status, significance, and positions.

4. Acquiesce to their decisions, opinions, preferences, plans and goals.

5. Actively serve their needs and desires without comment or complaint.
6. Admiration of their achievements, contribution, class, and stature.
7. Answerable for their mistakes and shortcomings; be their "fall guy."
8. Apologetic to calm them down when things don't go how they want.
9. Appease their moments of anger and irrationality, to reassure them.
10. Assist them to accomplish what they themselves cannot do alone.
11. Adapt to their mood swings, hostility, demands, and expectations.
12. Adopt their philosophy, perspective, approach, and methods as right.
13. Adhere to their rules, preferences, methods, strategies, and plans.
14. Accolades are due them, for directing others to achieve goals.
15. Admission of errors, so they can be corrected and punished.

Most people react to *Type A* behavior, expressing their feelings of:

1. Abandoned and discarded when less useful and exploitable than others.
2. Abased by insults, criticism, abuse, and hostility when venting off.

3. Admonished and threatened with losses and punishment if not right.
4. Aggravated by aggressive, demanding and unreasonable attitudes.
5. Agitated by increased conflict and stress level caused by demands.
6. Ambushed so they can get the upper hand and put others on defense.
7. Annoyed by constant criticism and wanting more as never satisfied.
8. Anguished by being better people, but exploited by their demands.
9. Abysmal and depressed feelings of powerlessness to change them.
10. Abhorrence to being forced to listen to them rant, rave, and rage.
11. Affronted by negativism, destructive criticism, blame, and accusations.
12. Aversion to being around them, but feeling obliged to tolerate them.
13. Avoidance when possible, without attracting their revengeful manner.

People recognize characteristics that ***Type A's* would deny**, such as:

1. Anality as expressed by asshole, ingrate, predatory personalities.
2. Arch-villainy from lack of compassion, and ability to hurt others.

3. Ancient worldview of self-aggrandizing despotic and tyrannical rule.

4. Arresting progress of others by sucking away their dreams and goals.

5. Attitude of superiority, braggadocios, and entitlement to get more.

6. Altercation whenever things don't go their way as fast as they demand.

7. Annihilation of their enemies, cohorts, and friends if obstacles to goals.

8. Assiduous speech and toxic, predatory, manipulative relationships.

9. Assigning hard work to others, as they relax, criticize and get credit.

10. Atomic and explosive fits of venom, rage, and irrationality when angry.

11. Austere and overly serious, boorish and envious of others' enjoyment.

12. Axing, cutting, and destroying people's lives in order to get self ahead.

13. Awful self-serving character and personality who could back stab well.

14. Archetype boss or enemy who others would love to avoid or destroy

15. Axiomatic view of world, that others must be wrong, as they are right.

16. Alter-ego is a spoiled and demanding nine-year-old brat with nine lives who never learned how to ask, but insist on their way or throws fits.

Type A people eventually carve out profitable, influential, and leadership positions in society because most people do not have the desire and stamina to confront, challenge and defeat these persistent, demanding, determined, and predatory *"Alphas." Type A* people push others to achieve, in order for the so-called *Alphas* to accumulate the benefits of other people's work. *Type A's* often take the attitude that people are lucky to be able to serve them, lucky to have a job that is provided by businesses owned or managed by *Type A's. Type A* CEOs have no loyalty to their employees, and will bankrupt their firms
by pulling out all the cash, and leaving a shell company with bankrupt employee pension funds.

Types As, while not necessary evil by nature, are usually evil by tendency, practices, attitude and behavior. They are cold-blooded and have no trouble moving up into leadership positions by backstabbing others, and stepping up on the backs of subordinates. Once they show the "backbone" to push away or eliminate their competitors, they are noticed and hired by other greed Type A's, who made it up the corporate ladder the same way, a processed called "earning one's stripes." Jesus Christ referred to these cold-blooded greedy and ambitious
Type A people as,"hypocrites... snakes... brood of vipers." [Matthew 23:29-33]. Cold-blooded reptilians also have voracious sexual appetites, having sex and procreating, without establishing relationships, responsibilities or loyalties. Primates on the other hand, are usually loyal, monogamous and establish parental responsibility for raising their young.

Type A leadership in the world has historically created conflict, violence and war because they are aggressive and insist on winning at all cost. The history of mankind is filled with plunder, rape, and murder at the direction and execution of *Type A's*. Of course, they rarely do their own dirty work, because they are accustomed to giving orders to their cohorts and underlings, and demand total submission and allegiance, which they refuse to do for anyone. *Type A* personalities are living contradictions, and are hypocrites, expecting others to do what they themselves do not do. Most victims of *Type A* predators don't ever forget their experience, but these *"Alphas"* don't feel they're doing anything wrong. They feel justified in exploiting others as instruments to pursue their selfish agendas because they feel superior and entitled to lead.

A better strategy would be for non-*Type A's* to unite in business endeavors, and using their superior creativity to *Type A's*, to challenge them in the free market place, and kick their ass. *Type A*'s need to get their asses kicked, so they can feel and understand how it feels to be humbled. But then, most *Type A*'s would only see challenges to their position as temporary, and then muster their resources for revenge. *Type A* people never seem to go away. They put stress on others, causing other people to die prematurely, while they seem to live on and on off the blood of those who are sacrificed.

The best advice to non-aggressive people is to avoid *Type A's* whenever possible, because their natural tendency and orientation is to take advantage of people, by any means necessary. *Type A's* are unlikely to ever change their ways, because this world structure has been designed by *Type A* people for the benefit of *Type A* people. All others beware *Type A* predators! In conclusion, the terrorist mindset is often rooted in Type A personality disorders where destructive action is the natural instinctive reaction to obstacles, frustrations, grudges and other challenges that block the attainment of their hidden goals – to feel their personal lives are better than others.

The Global Planting of the Seeds of Terrorism

Part 1: Who First Planted The Seeds of Terrorism in the Third World?

On September 11, 1973, an orchestrated coup allegedly supported by the US overthrew the elected socialist but legitimate coalition government of Salvador Allende in Chile, and installed the repressive anti-communist military regime of General Pinochet. Almost thirty years later, on 9-11-2001, terrorists who were trained by Americans as "resistance fighters", who had previously fought against the Soviet Union's communist expansionism in Afghanistan, invaded America, and subjected us to the worse single terrorist act on soil, since the Army wiped out the Native Americans. The seeds of terrorism were planted in the Third World by imperialists and colonialists, supposed practitioners of Christianity, despite the fact that the Bible forbids killing. It should be no surprise that these seeds have over the centuries set deep roots in the hearts and minds of those who continue to feel exploited by western capitalism and power, particularly among poor Moslems who become recruited for jihad against the West and America.

Besides a common history of foreign domination, economic exploitation, and political/military rule during periods of imperialism, colonization, and neo-colonialism, a majority of Third World nations have shared the plight of impoverished, uneducated, and powerless populaces. During historical periods of exploitations by foreigners or neo-colonialist puppet governments, the countries of the Third World were raped of their natural and human resources to satisfy the North's greed and need for raw materials and cheap or slave labor.

Subsequent to WW2, and the global independence movements that ensued, the "First World" changed its economic strategies of dominance and control, by using the World Bank, and IMF to burden developing economies with high interest loans, and forced economic restructuring (SAPs) or "structural adjustment plans" on developing countries, while corrupt neo-colonialist governments, military juntas, and regimes comprised of foreign, transplanted, and indigenous cohorts banked the loans with little trickling down to those in greatest need of help.

Third World workers toiled hard for meager and subsistence wages to export generally a few national commodities, usually owned by foreign companies, who profited over 100 times what was paid to workers. In return, the First World exported manufactured goods to Third World nations at greatly inflated prices that in general, only the elites or small middle classes in their poor countries could afford. Since it was rare for workers in less developed post-colonialist nations to usurp power from their elitist

Neo-colonial governments, the economic and political interests and rights of the working class, peasants, women, and children were ignored. When a few true revolutions succeeded, it came at a great cost in human lives to the masses, and generally resulted in the North imposing economic sanctions that kept newly emerging nations relatively poor and powerless in the international economy.

Part 2: What Role Did the U.S. Contribute to Planting the Seeds of Terrorism?

The U.S. has had a long history of international spying and some alleged wrong doings since WW2. However, it's primary focus during the Cold War was spying on the USSR (the former Soviet Union) and the P.R.C. (formerly "Red China"), and also concentrated on destabilizing Asian and Latin American national liberation movements that had "leftist" or communist leanings, as part of the political policy to keep the Western Hemisphere and Southeast Asia free of communist and socialist "expansion".

In the zealous pursuit of perceived national policies, the trained, funded, and supplied arms to military juntas, national police, paramilitary and neo-fascist groups all over the world, in attempting to identify, capture, torture, and assassinate persons who were perceived to be leftist organizers, politicians, supporters, and sympathizers. Abundant use was made of field agents from corrupt local right wing groups and individuals who served the interests of the property class in their fight to maintain political and economic dominance over the working class and peasants. Using local recruits, US agents were able to infiltrate and subterfuge leftist labor and political groups who were attempting to assert their basic rights to recognition, fair treatment, and inclusion in their regional or national governance structure.

During these campaigns of terror, thousands of innocent and decent people were tortured and killed without remorse, and often for no purpose other than for the sick entertainment of death squads gone wild. In addition, disinformation campaigns to discredit and frame various leftist leaders resulted in their detainment, torture, and murder. When leftist governments were not perceived as being friendly to American strategic interests, agents secretly sponsored the overthrow of legitimate governments that were popularly elected or supported. The military coups often replaced left-leaning regimes with corrupt elitist right wing juntas whose pledge against communism and socialism were sufficient collateral equity to justify abundant economic, military, and political rewards from America. In more recent times, the support of Arab Spring rebellions resulted in the unintended consequence of handing radical Islam more power.

Part 3: How Have Terrorists Activities Affected American Citizens?

Post WW2 Americans fell into a long period of national pride, arrogance, egocentrism, and escapist fantasies that discounted the needs of the world. They depended upon their elected government to deal with international affairs, and were enjoying the post-war baby boom. Not until the failures of the Vietnam War and the disgraceful resignation of Nixon, did average citizens realize they trusted their government too much, that their sons, brothers, and fathers had died in foreign lands for uncertain reasons, or for no good reasons. Many Americans began to believe their government regularly lied to them, and had held them in contempt for treating the electorate as the ignorant, easily manipulated, and foolishly naive silent majority.

The consequence of misdeeds and government cover-ups that became exposed in many unethical or bungled operations, including Brazil, Panama, Nicaragua, Uruguay, Chile, and many other countries caused American citizens to doubt and distrust the wisdom and tactics of their government. Citizens were again forced and shaken out of their general malaise by the WTC terrorists holocaust of 9-11-01, to suddenly reap the lessons of engagement errors in the Middle East, Central Asia, and East Asia. Much of the training of leaders in most present-day terrorist groups to the techniques of subterfuge, secrecy, spying, infiltration, and sabotage owe their knowledge to Americans. Now, the seeds of destruction are being turned back on our own citizens, who are jumping on the bandwagon of patriotism, but with trepidation, fear, and uncertainty. Consequently, average loyal American citizens who only wish to live a decent life in a more or less free society can no longer do that without fear.

Who should we blame for creating the environment where over a third of our citizens become afraid to open their mail, fly on jets, go to the shopping mall, or attend large public events? Who should we blame for the logical consequences of state-sponsored terrorism that now threatens to imprison our population in emotional and physical cocoons that cannot guarantee any real sense of security? The seeds of violence eventually grow into the roots of violence, which become the trunks of rebellion. Then one day, the branches sprout countless leaves that fall to the ground, laced with poison. That's what Americans are now experiencing, the consequences of previous state-sponsored terrorism coming home to roost.

Part 4: How Does the Third World Feel About Terrorism?

U.S. operations have generally acted to thwart the will of the people in nations subjected to their subterfuge, as it initiated, coordinated, financed, and directed field agents to assassinate leftist leaders, disrupt labor organizations, bomb buildings, and kill thousands of innocent people. The U.S. trained military and paramilitary groups, death squads, and terrorists to act as neo-colonialist armies that backed corrupt regimes, which usually did not represent the will of the people being ruled. Instead, rule was forced upon nations and peoples, with the economic and political agendas of the U.S. as the primary motive and justification. The economic and political disruptions to other nations caused the masses great suffering, starvation, suffering and death, as neo-colonialist military juntas were installed to oppress the masses and their desire for national liberation and alignment with socialist states.

The negative consequences of U.S. involvement and manipulation of the domestic affairs of other nations gave rise to deep-rooted anger, resentment, and hatred for the U.S. and by association, all Americans. It is no surprise that Americans and their corporate and government symbols are under attack all over the Third World, and now on home soil in America. During WW2, the United States of America was loved and viewed by the world's peoples as the "Great Liberator", freedom fighters, and supporters of the oppressed masses. Since the Vietnam War, military and U.S.

operations in Latin America, Africa, and S.E. Asia have greatly tarnished and even negated the noble image of America, the torch for freedom. The vast majority of masses in the Third World now almost universally view America as supporters of the corrupt financiers of oppression, uncaring of the plight of the suffering, and at worse are regarded as terrorists and mass murders.

The effects of European and American expansionism, imperialism, and colonialism were horrific in the Third World. Conquered and colonized lands became devastated in terms of the wanton rape of their natural resources and inhumane exploitation of cheap or slave labor. Third World families, tribes, civilizations, and cultures were completely uprooted, decimated, or destroyed in the name of capitalism and Manifest Destiny.

The inhumane treatment of Third World peoples was justified by whites as God's will, because white men were made in the image of God. It was consequently the white man's role to have dominion over colored peoples who were obviously not made in the image of the monotheistic God, who could only be white. Colonized people were viewed as less than human, as uncivilized savages who needed to be dominated, controlled, and exploited. Changing savages from their indigenous ways to adopt Christian values and western culture was seen as "the white man's burden".

Hundreds of years of colonialism and often-barbarous conduct on the part of colonialists acted to institutionalize western corporate dominance. However, arrogant and exploitive western behavior caused a deep-rooted resentment and hatred of the West that still widely persist in the Third World in present times. Periphery economies were changed from agrarian to industrial, and massive population migrations, seeking employment, essentially abandoned the remnants of traditional agrarian, tribal, familial, cultural, and community-oriented societies. Like mirrors of the West, indigenous people flocked to urban centers of production and trade, to become faceless clogs in the wheels of industrial production and commercial enterprises, all of which were owned by domestic and international elites.

The rift between the great fortunes of western exploitation, and the residual wealth left in the periphery was quickly usurped and controlled by indigenous elites who, supported by the center, formed corrupt neo-colonialist governments to protect western assets by oppressing the masses. The outcome of imperialism, colonialism, and neo-colonialism on the Third World was poverty, powerlessness, hopelessness, and destitute. Consequently, revolutionary sentiments and national liberation movements sprang up in the periphery, which were generally thwarted by military and paramilitary campaigns directed, financed, and armed by the First World. Under the dominant world system of gross inequities between the rich versus the poor, the powerful versus the powerless, "freedom fighters" perceive their role as noble, especially in their "manifest destiny" as soldiers for their religious beliefs. They feel compelled to kill as many westerners as possible; particularly Americans who they view are the primary exploiters and oppressors. Like the Japanese Kamikazes of World War 2, the terrorists who are spread out all over the world, feel they have a divine purpose in death. They hate us, even more than we despise the terrible things that they've done to us.

Part 5: How Will Globalization of Monopolistic Capitalism Affect Terrorism?

The era of "defensive monopoly capitalism", described in the book *Global Rift* appears to be giving way to "second-coming" capitalism, a reversion that mirrors conditions and precedents of "monopoly capitalism". Second-coming capitalism focuses our attention to the retrenchment from humane treatment of workers, and a return to viewing people as commodities in a global capitalistic marketplace. The major difference is, while under monopoly capitalism, labor exploitation was primarily confined to the Third World; however, under second-coming capitalism, there are no such distinctions on geographic or cultural boundaries. Second-coming capitalism reverses the small but significant gains made by workers in their relationship with the owners of production. Even in the First World, workers are being abandoned for the sake of maintaining advantages in the international flow of capital and the globalization of capital assets by MNCs, multi-national corporations, owned by the global Elites.

No longer do employers and industrial equity owners feel morally obligated by relationships and loyalties. Serfs and slaves were "cared for" by owners and employers even during times of low production, low profit, and economic losses. During the "industrial capitalism" era, employers allowed wages to be high enough to permit workers to become customers of the products of industry, thereby creating a stable demand for products, with resultant steady corporate profits. Second-coming capitalism has no such loyalties or responsibilities. It searches for the cheapest labor markets for production; it extracts the greatest amounts of natural resources utilizing technologies that efficiently replace millions of manual laborers; it shifts to high-tech corporate farming to eliminate once large numbers of human harvesters; it's rapidly replacing technology workers with computers and new technologies, and replacing natural commodities with synthetically manufactured substitutes. The techniques of monopolistic capitalism by institutionalized neo-colonialism are now being applied globally against the world's working class, regardless of jurisdiction in the First or Third Worlds.

World governments are capitulating to the naked orientation of global capitalism, as MNC's push for privatization of governments, and pure profit motive drives global equity owners to seek membership in the WTO. Financing international commerce has more to do with obtaining credit from the World Bank and IMF than in domestic or regional trade agreements. As greedy capitalists shed their "burden" for the working class, in the pursuit of wanton and unregulated profits, many CEOs earn over 1,000 times the average worker's wage, and then make massive layoffs, not to increase shareholder dividends, but to protect and increase CEO benefits and profits. It is becoming increasingly clear that the push for the once elusive "one world government" global empire ascribed to by the Romans is rapidly taking form in second-coming capitalism, as the global Elites attempt to wrestle final control of the world from the people by making the masses obsolete. Timothy McVey, Oklahoma Bomber and Terrorist is among the first wave of domestic working class terrorists who will spring forth from every nation on earth, whose depth and breath will make the al-Qaeda terrorist network look like boy scouts.

Part 6: Historical Contexts, Current Trends, and Possible or Probable Future Events

The Past:

The history of the world has always been the struggle for dominance between the powerful and the relatively powerless. A dynamic life and death balance occurs at all levels of life, from viruses to humans, just as it had once existed among dinosaurs and earliest life. Is mankind's problems part of natural selection? Has the hand of divine intervention been no more than an innate human desire for benevolent paternalism? And if so, is the human desire to believe in gods or a monotheistic God based on a psychological fear of the harsh environment that has always been naturally filled with violence and danger over time? And if there is a superior intelligent entity as God, why should that presumption exclude the existence of lesser gods, defined as intelligent living beings that are superior to humans? If God exist, why isn't it at least probable that humans have been, continue to be, and will in the future be visited by gods, not all of whom want to embrace and love humans, but rather to dominate us, as perhaps in the past?

Simple math and science relative to cosmology indicate the Earth is no more than 5.5 billion years old, orbiting a lesser star, the sun, in the outer quadrant of the Milky Way, a lesser galaxy in the outer quadrant of a visible universe that is 12-15 billion years old. Primates that may be relatives to humans appeared on earth about a mere 4.5 million years ago. The visible universe contains over 100 billion galaxies, each containing 100 to 200 billion stars. We are infants in the scope of time, in the breath of life. Once again, our ethnocentrism tries to justify that we are the center of intelligent life, yet human history and contemporary affairs has repeatedly proven that we are not very intelligent, and definitely not particularly wise or humane as a species. What other species makes it a routine activity to kill its own kind in massive numbers, and to exterminate millions of other species, whether deliberately or inconsiderately?

Viewed from space, humans are like a disease, overrunning and killing everything, animals, plants, and the ecosystem. And we feel justified, a manifest destiny to spread our need to explore and dominate into space, and to other planets. And what will humans likely do, should we finally figure out how to get "there"? Probably the same program as we have on Earth; plunder, exploit, extract, destroy, and kill anything that gets in the way, just as the program against the Third World has been effected since Europe's boom days in exploration led to imperialism, colonialism, neo-colonialism, and now globalization. How close we are to global thermal nuclear war is a subject of debate and secret preparations by paranoid governments who attempt to protect their assets from other states and "terrorists." Perhaps the smallest life forms, the bacteria will reclaim the Earth from humans, by catastrophic plague from which no known anti-biotic is effective. That might be a good thing for the planet, though not good for Homo sapiens.

Since the development of city-states evolved into nation-states, various forms of government were created to give dominance and economic advantage to U.S. classes of humans. In the quest and justification for social order and peace, states have gone to war thousands of times, killing over a billion people in history. Empires, kingdoms, and dynasties still exist, but in modern form, renamed with more eloquent terms, like democracy and socialism. The U.S. 10% of humans still own or control 90% of the land and resources of our planet, and in too many cases, that includes ownership of human beings as slaves, serfs, and indentured servants who are exploited at low wages, for crime, or prostitution to enrich the coffers of their "employers". No matter what nation we look at, the game is the same, only names have changed.

The Present:

The rich exploit the poor. The poor are too busy trying to survive meager lives to organize for better rights, as they've become sheep for slaughter, afraid of the wolves, the police, paramilitary, and military whose primary job is to protect the equity owners in their respective nations, and not to protect people. Only a fool would feel more secure, when as a commercial jetliner passenger, one sees the jet fighter escorts off its wing tips. The escorts' job is to shoot down the commercial jet, should there "appear" to be a threat the jet "might" be used instead as a bomb. Suicidal "terrorists" or deranged individuals care little if they are killed in the course of acting out their agenda against the public, because a glorified death is their primary goal. Oftentimes, deranged people or terrorists just want their "fifteen minutes of fame" as their personal revenge for their feelings of powerlessness, hopelessness, and extreme hatred.

If the role of military jets is now to shoot down commercial jets, then every passenger should be issued parachutes and briefed on their use as part of boarding and emergency information dispensed by flight attendants. But that would cost too much for airlines. Once again, a price has been placed on human life, so the common religious thought that human life is precious and priceless is a lie, otherwise its followers would practice that value. The scientists are probably more realistic in stating that a human being's trace elements are worth less than ten dollars in carbon compounds. Or maybe a convicted felon from a Chinese prison is worth the cost of his transplantable body parts, which to that convict or political prisoner becomes a negative incentive, worth a couple of hundred dollars to the state, and a quicker death to the incarcerated.

And now, we have a czar of homeland security in America. We should know that any bureaucracy that has ever been created is likely to grow, to usurp more power, and to jealously guard their jurisdiction. The history of organizational behavior indicate that its actors will refuse to relinquish power and budget, once its been granted. What will the evolution of homeland security become? Will citizens be required to organize "building watch", "school watch", and "job watch" as a more pervasive and ominous form of present day voluntary "neighborhood watch"? How did the "SS" begin in pre-WW2 Germany? Perhaps citizens, for "their own protection" will be required to carry "national identification cards", a "smart-card" with intrusive personal, financial, and medical information, encoded and assessable only to banks, insurance companies, and the government. And what comes after the "smart card"? Bio-computer chip implants? Why not? After all, it's a bitter pill to swallow, but the "chip" will be for our own good. Right?

We need to look no further than recent history to see the effects of state-sponsored terrorism, mass-based reactive terrorism, and individually based Kamikaze terrorism. The seeds of rebellion and terrorism have been planted by state-sponsored or supported terrorism that is the common legacy of imperialism, colonialism, neo-colonialism, and corrupt regimes. There are no "truly innocent" parties, and no "true victims" in acts of terrorism. Neither non-combatants nor military personnel can claim neutrality. To the degree that citizens benefit, however slightly, from the economic, political, and military policies of states that oppress other people, they become accomplices and are no longer "innocent" of the consequences of such policies. There is no "innocence" to the logical and predictable consequences and rebellion that invariably and inevitably result as desperate reactions to oppression and great economic disparities.

The Future:

So how is the world going to get out of this latest round of terrorism? Will "smoking out terrorist", and "getting them on the run" truly solve the root causes of terrorism? Or will harsh military and economic policies and disparate globalization serve to galvanize a new and even deadlier generation of suicidal religious zealots? The "kill ratio" of 20 terrorists was about 3,000 in the WTC incident of 9-11-01. If 2,000 terrorists can sustain that rate, and then 300,000 people could be killed. If 20,000 terrorists, then 3,000,000 people could die (half the number of people murdered during the Holocaust). If 200,000 jihadists can reproduce that rate, then 30,000,000 people could be killed. But we're only talking about flying jets into skyscrapers and using IEDs. Bio-terrorism or nuclear terrorism would undoubtedly up the ante and "kill ratio". Maybe that's part of a secret plan.

The survival of mankind will depend on fundamentally changing the elitist global system that supports and enforces the grossly inequitable distribution of economic resources to the great suffering of the poor. But will the rich voluntarily give up their power and wealth? Never. But might the Elites consider paradigm changes if it could be proven that their short term, and especially long-term need for social and political stability could be better served by changing specific facets of the world system? Possibly yes, if it could improve the profits of the wealthy multi-national and indigenous elites.

Impending global paradigm changes can be seen on the event horizon that will alter the manner in which humans related to each other, and how nation-states deal with the global village, and its own domestic affairs. The possible outcomes are many, and the extreme consequences could either be human extinction, or human enlightenment, nuclear and genetic war killing billions of people, or consensual interaction and engagement leading to long lasting peace and prosperity for all. Or there may be "external" extraterrestrial forces that will create a complete realignment of human perceptions and values, whether that would be in the form of an "Armageddon" sized asteroid or returning of the "gods", no one can predict. We shall know, when we know.

The impending paradigm changes are many, cross several disciplines, and will invariably have interactive effects on almost all aspects of life. Elitism versus powerlessness has been institutionalized and woven into cultures as class, racism, ethnic bias, religious intolerance, sex and gender have resulted in great suffering and poverty for exploited and debased people. Governance and organizational structure and power have been hierarchical, centralized, and unequal instead of decentralized, horizontally multi-tiered, and consensual that encourages power sharing instead of concentration. The world economic system is based on pure profit, with little or no regards for resource depletion or inhumane exploitation and disparities. The Elites' vision of a completely integrated global market, controlled by a relatively small group of MNC's, owned by a handful of Elites, who in collusion control every nation-state on the planet, is a twisted idea based on wanton greed and profiteering from other peoples' grief. It is unclear at what point the masses will rebel, or whether they may acquiesce to authority, as in the United States. It is unclear if the Elites will someday unleash their technological and military might to kill 4 billion poor people, to "cleanse" the world of poverty, leaving a world with a dichotomy, those inhabitants who rule, and those who purpose is to serve those who rule.

Technological advances are even now pushing the envelope in science and will impact global social, political, military and economic systems in a wide range of areas within the next decade. New sources of renewable energy, genetic manipulation, "clean" weapons of mass destruction, extra-low-frequency (ELF) mind-control methods, climatic disruptions or control, and space exploration will pressure the status quo to adjust and to integrate the impending changes into their global system of profiteering. Will the result be greater control of the minds, hearts, and souls of human beings? Or will something better emerge? I hope the later, but if history is a teacher, then I fear the former. Let's hope for a quantum improvement in the quality of life, with an increase in purpose, and a de-emphasis on materialism and consumerism. Let's pray for peace and stability through education and empowerment, to prevent future violence and wars.

Part 7: The Elitist Plan to Make the Working Class Obsolete

The world is undergoing great transition and transformations that have and continues to change the relationships between nation-states, cultures, peoples, races, religions, and classes. The old paradigm of "wealth makes power, and might makes right" is increasingly being challenged by those seeking a paradigm shift to "people make might, makes right". Over two-thirds of the world's population are impoverished, and have little hope for improving their lives, not within their life times, nor their children's lifetimes. The poor look to desperate measures to make relatively small gains, yet the Elites refuse to allow any significant challenge to their world system's dichotomy of power and wealth.

The Elites feel compelled to retain their total dominance and control over the world's resources and peoples, and they refuse to power share or relinquish even a small portion of their power. The Elites fear that once the masses develop a liking for the sweet taste of power and wealth, they will wrestle it from the Elites. Are the masses no more moral or less greedy than the Elites, given the opportunities? From the egocentric and self-justifying perspectives of the Elites, it is the Elites who are of higher morality and humanity than the masses. And it is the Elites who are ordained and deserving to rule the world.

The Elites believe that the masses are unfit to rule. Let the masses eat gruel. Keep the faceless masses oppressed and minimally subsisting, to rob them of their energy and will to live. And let the masses die off, to correct the overpopulation and ecological pollution problems. The Elites' arrogance blinds them to the swelling desire for empowerment by the oppressed, which the world is only beginning to see since the terrorism of 9-11-01. And the Elites' power lust makes their hearts hard, even as they mourn for their own. Where will the impending clash between the interests of the rich versus the poor lead our world? Will progressive enlightenment become the new paradigm, or shall mankind fall into a deep abyss? The following section of opined predictions attempts to project potential scenarios of the impending events over the next decade in human evolution, or devolution. There is no way to really know, but without substantive changes to the world system, chaos will persist, and as long as world conflicts exist, the global powder keg can explode at any time.

Part 8: Historical and Possible Chronology for Global Genocide

1980s: Robotics introduced to auto building assembly lines, resulting in higher efficiency, but drastically decreasing the number of higher paid workers. Corporate executive incomes average 100 times that of average workers. Surveillance technology is becoming more popular as a crime prevention tool.

1990s: Cell phone explosion revolutionizes communications potential. Voice recognition technology improving, allowing vocal email recognition. Proliferation of ISPs and free email supports a boom in the dotcom sector. The pre-Y2K hype pumps half a trillion dollars into the technology market as the "fix", encouraging uncontrolled stock market speculation by average citizens, boosting the value of stocks duringY2K. Surveillance technology becomes more pervasive as it becomes miniaturized.

2000: Interactive voice recognition phone trees replace receptionists, phone operators, and customer service representatives for major corporations. PCs increase processing speed by a factor of 40 times within 10 years and chip memory quadruples [squared] to 128K. Digital data transmission speed and bandwidth and fiber optics greatly increase the limits communications. The dot com crash sucked half a trillion dollars out of retirement funds, and leaves the average retiree more broke than before Y2K.

2008: As the world begins to slip into an economic recession, terrorists strike at the heart of the world's financial center, setting back the economy for several months. As the mighty American-British Armada strike at the few assets of one of the poorest and most desolate nation-states in the world, terrorists retaliate against owned or supported targets all over the world. The nations of the North respond defensively, and follow the American program of "homeland defense". Border controls are tightened. Citizens allow greater surveillance, search, and arrest powers to the state, further limiting constitutional protections. Economic markets are on a roller coaster ride.

2012: New investment opportunities expand in security, pharmaceutical, and military technologies. A new generation of surveillance, eavesdropping, sniffing, testing, and "early warning" systems become available to corporations, government, and individuals who can afford them. The world economy stabilizes as incidents of terrorism decreases, and appears to be under control. A few incidents of car bombings, but nothing major, but there's no lasting peace between Israel and Palestine. Russia's economy still suffers and resentment against the West increase, as billions of economic aid never reach the impoverished masses.

2015: Coordinated biological terrorist attacks via the mail are attempted by terrorists, killing several hundreds of thousands of people. The populace is warned in time to avert higher numbers of deaths. Intelligence information suggests Iran as the supplier of the biological weapons. The U.S. fails to gain the support of the Arab world for military action, and the US-Israel-NATO allies, against the wishes of the UN, and unilaterally bombs Iran's military facilities, taking out his biological, chemical, and nuclear capacity. A power vacuum arises in Iran, and the U.S. repatriates half of the thousands of Iranians who have been living in the to set up a puppet government in Iran.

2016: The Syrians feel they are next on the hit list. On the surface, they pretend to cooperate with Russia, in exchange for economic aid. Surreptitiously, they support various groups who wish to destabilize the U.S. and Israel. They make secret deals with certain rouge KGB agents and individuals in the Russian crime syndicates to purchase nuclear weapons. Our intelligence network discovers the plot. A secret plan is made to retrieve the nukes. When Special Forces fail to recover all of the nukes, and several teams are captured or killed the/NATO pact strike Syria, then install a puppet government. To prevent future terrorism, all citizens are mandated to carry national identification "smart cards" in all "free trade" nations who are signatories to the WTO.

2017: Great strides are made in stem cell research and the first human being is successfully cloned (after several dozen failed and deformed fetuses are disposed). A complete head transplant is made, and stem cells permit the reattachment of the spinal nerves. Chris Reeves regains his ability to function without machine assistance. Cold fusion and essentially frictionless gravity propelled technologies prove to be feasible, causing a new boom in energy investments. Big oil interests attempt to block the new technology, but it is bigger than big oil, which then attempts to retool and reinvest in new wave energies. The North controls the oil production in Iraq, Iran, and Syria. The Saudi's and other oil producers capitulate to Northern price controls, and see their wealth decrease drastically due to new energy sources.

2019: An international team, comprised of an American, Brit, German, Russian, and Chinese orbit Mars. Evidence of possible subterranean intelligent civilizations is suppressed. Developed nations convert to new energies, while developing nations are sold the oil from the Middle East. Big Oil earns even more profits, with one foot in each energy technology, old and new. Another quantum leap in computer miniaturization, processing speed, and memory permits the development of wristwatch sized voice activated computers with global wireless connection. People can walk, see, talk, and understand anyone with a similar device anywhere on our Planet. The world continues to become more dichotomous, as the economic differences between the rich and the poor is exacerbated, in both the North and South. The scientific community leaks secret photos showing remnants of Martian life and civilizations.

2020: The First World optical fiber network is in place and secured, and data transmission speed increases by 1000x due to the global optic fiber network. Voice recognition linked to robotics equipment has been miniaturized as intelligent multi-functional "slaves." Millions of workers' have their jobs replaced by computer and robotics technologies. Citizens in developed nations are hard pressed to find jobs, and they fall into hard times. The world falls into a deep economic recession and regional depression, with worldwide rebellion.

2021: Civil unrest in the North increase, commensurate with mass insurrection in Third World puppet states, as unemployed, suffering, and impoverished masses seek to attack the symbols of the Elites. The North mandates all employed citizens to take the computer "low-jack" implant as a strategy to control insurrection. The Elites release a secret genetically engineered food-borne virus into genetically modified foods. Those who agreed to receive the "low-jack" chip are able to obtain untreated food from special government regulated stores or delivery services. The food virus has an incubation period of 6 months, and 4 billion people become suspiciously infected. Symptoms include loss of appetite, vomiting, and general malaise. Death occurs due to starvation. It's non-infective to non-consumers, but the UN and nations of the North give infected foods as humanitarian aid all over the world.

2021: A singular world government is established by the North to coordinate the "fight against disease", and they pretend to be feverishly working on a cure for the food virus, now dubbed "poor man's disease". The secret vaccine is locked in government safes. Two billion people die in the Third World after the 6 months incubation period. No cure is in sight. The international team lands on Mars, and begin exploration and colonization.

2022: The One World Government state a cure for "poor man's disease" is close at hand, but another 2 billion people die during the first six months of the year, after which the miracle "cure" is released to the public. The genetically engineered food virus is withheld from the food chain. The world's population stands at 2.5 billion people, of which 1 billion reside relative disease free in the

North (comprised of 95% whites), 500 million in White Russia, Middle East, and Central Asia, 500 million in China, Japan, India, and advanced Asian nations. The remainder 450 million people inhabit Latin America, and less than 50 million are still alive in Africa. The One World Government divides the territories in Africa into reconstruction zones, to exploit its virgin territories for expansive mineral deposits and natural resources.

2025: As the world begins to recover its economic balance, with a reduced, but more efficient economic distribution system, most industrial assets remain in place. Among the Elites, few were affected by "poor man's disease", and they continue to rule their nation-states. They negotiate and cooperate among each other for the planned utilization of planetary resources, both human, non-human, and inanimate. The elitist paradigm of a global economy with exclusive control of resource exploitation and distribution by the One World Government that serves the one million global U.S. is finally achieved. The rest of humanity is controlled and coerced to serving the wishes of the Elites, and anyone who objects, whether through speech or press, is imprisoned and "re-educated" through high-tech mind-control and brain-reprogramming techniques, or they are "recycled" as molecules for the new technologies.

2029: In the course of exploiting deep into Africa's subsoil in search of minerals needed for high tech computers, robotics, and space exploration, an unknown bacteria is released that is highly transmittable and persistent through air, liquids, and solids. The bacteria's rapid spread is sudden and unabated. Private labs took an entire week to diagnose it as a new biological agent, but by that time, 2 billion people die, including half of the one million ruling U.S. The rest of humanity's existence hangs in the balance. Mankind is only a week from extinction. Several hundred babies are born at the last moments as humans take their last dying breaths.

From the heavens, UFO's appear. The "ETs" are able to communicate with the ancient bacteria colonies through nano-molecules that are encoded with chemical markers that the bacteria manipulate. The ETs ask the killer bacteria why they killed off the human species, and the bacteria replied that humans were "evil", a rogue species only interested in consuming and destruction of all life on the planet. The bacteria felt that they had no more use for human hosts because they had already spread competing species of bacteria all over the world, creating conflict, violence, and war among trillions and trillions of bacterial colonies, which was upsetting the balance of life at the primal stages of life. The ET's acknowledge, and they take the last vestiges of the human species into their spacecrafts and fly off into ouster space.

2030: The plants and animals on planet Earth begin again to replenish the world. Natural forces again respond to a dynamic balance once lost to humans. Once populated human cities, state symbols, great air forces, and naval armadas become wreckage and is recycled as shelter for animals, birds, and sea creatures. Vegetation eventually overgrows even the highest skyscrapers. From space, the planet appears serene, as a revolving multi-colored sphere, once again as it had previously been for billions of years.

Back to 2013: Then again, there could be other scenarios that could resolve world problems by dealing realistically with the root causes of violence, which are disempowerment, poverty, intolerance, and fanaticism. Each is a cause of the other, as powerlessness is usually expresses by impoverishment, which in turn abets intolerance and a rise of fanaticism, whether based on religious or political ideology. The root of all evils in human history can be traced directly or indirectly to the wanton greed and hoarding of power by the Elites of the world. Until the Elites are willing to relent in their avarice, the masses in the world will feel justified in attacking elitist symbols and nation-states by any means necessary. And the Elites and their great militaries will feel justified to respond in kind, eventually leading to mass genocide.

A great American pacifist civil rights leader once had a vision, which has turned out to be a plead... he had a dream that someday, human beings of all races could live together in peace and brotherhood. Later, another commoner, after being brutally beat by police, asked his community, "Why can't we just get along"? Both of these men were named King, and for a brief moment in time, they were the people's kings. It's a shame that too many people choose to submit to the authority of ordained kings, and not enough submit to the wisdom of their own people's kings. We could have a better world if the Elites will arrests their perverse program of world domination and total global exploitation. The consequences are grave, not only for the masses, but also eventually for the world's Elites, and for the Homo sapiens.

Chapter 2 – The Strategies

We see the US as being the leader, and broker of international coalitions from the U.N., to NATO, to "Desert Storm", to the "war on terrorism." If any nation can police the world and push historical antagonists into a peace settlement in the Middle East, it would most likely be the US because it is the hegemon, the most powerful nation in the history of the world, militarily and economically.

Let me use an analogy. The US is like the head of a neighborhood gang, when threatened by bullies from other neighborhoods, he rallies his gang together to fight the other neighborhoods. The US concept of "gang" is not meant in a disparaging manner, only that the analogy serves to illuminate the process of leadership and self interests in global relations. The fight against other "gangs" and neighborhoods could be economic sanctions, military actions, or monetary prohibitions. While the US needs the support of his gang members, he acts quite the leader by encouraging, pressuring, bribing, promising, bartering, negotiating, and even secretly acquiescing on certain issues to key members, to obtain support for directed actions, that respond primarily to interests.

Why do other gang members go along with the gang leader? Because no one else is tough enough to beat him, and no one else has sufficient resources and talent to defend against the leader once a crisis is over. The gang must go along with the leader, or suffer the consequences afterwards, as history has already proven that many times. In addition, after a crisis is resolved, and the bullies in other neighborhoods are put in their place, his gang members regain a sense of security in knowing they can travel outside their neighborhood without fear of attack or reprisal. The international arena is basically anarchic, uncertain, and unpredictable. Bringing and maintaining order and stability to an anarchic world can only fall to the hegemon. At one time, the top dog was Britain, who after the ravages of WW2, passed the torch to its Anglo cousin, FDR's America.

One of the privileges of being the top dog is to be able to break agreements, without sanctions from the rest of the gang, and while the rest of the gang individually mutters and whines, no single person dares to take action against the leader. As long as each member gains sufficient benefits from accepting the leader's position, versus smaller inconveniences, no one is going to fight him if he wants the prettiest girl in the gang. The gang expects each member to forgive the leader for taking advantage of various situations, for breaking promises, for taking a larger share of profits, and for getting more, as compared to any other member. The gang has come to expect the top dog to get what he wants, because he can, and they need him to lead.

The U.S. government, as the international hegemonic power, can and does pretty much what it wants, as long as its power continues to appear legitimate to its electorate, and to its allies. In cases where American interests are served, the will go along with international conventions, but as soon as it feels its interests would

Be threatened, it will stand alone, without fear of reprisal or recrimination. Take for example the fact that the US was the only dissenting vote in the U.N. on the latest ecological convention against greenhouse gases. Even if the US was to sign such a convention, who is going to seriously reprimand the government, or join in economic or military reprisals against America if it were to break that, or any other treaty? Especially in the current political climate, anyone, any group, or any state that is against the U.S. is likely to be seen, at the very least, as a terrorist sympathizer.

During WW2, the government earned its preeminence by proving it had the ability to engender patriotism and unquestioned support of government policies by its citizens during times of crisis. The US also planted the seeds of economic imperialism by helping to rebuild Europe, Japan, and other post-colonial lands. If we look back at post-Nazi world history, most nations of the world are beholden to the U.S. for one thing or another, for American cash, industry, technology, liberation, modernization... something. Sure the CIA, as an instrument of foreign policy created conflict and helped to overthrow elected regimes that were viewed as unfavorable or hostile to U.S. interests, and 79 CIA agents have died serving American interests.

Since the international community owes the U.S. so much, it takes advantage from time to time, and tries to get the lion's share of what our world has to offer. Moreover, who dares to really challenge the United States of America? Just see what's happening to the Taliban right now, what happened to Iraq a decade earlier, and what happened to Sadam Hussein, Momar Gadhafi, Osama bin

Laden and other petty tyrants. No nation-state, group, or individuals in their right mind really wants to be on America's top "hit list", unless it has to do with music.

The bottom line is economic power, coupled with a powerful military, driven by technology, and supported by a patriotic (though somewhat misinformed or sometimes brainless) citizenry, allows the US to utilize various strategies, sometimes unfairly or illegitimately by international perspectives, to carry out policies that benefit those U.S. groups of domestic actors who exert the greatest influence on the government. When international situations threaten American hegemony, the US government steps in to protect corporate interests and to protect the American economy, whether the cause of disequilibria is oil prices, the nuclear arms race, or terrorism. And any benefits that the American power U.S. derives from the international system trickles down to the American masses, who as a group still enjoys one of the highest per capita incomes in the world (however, as the US economy becomes more bifurcated, the poor more increasingly takes on attributes typically ascribed to Third World populations).

Who can fight against all that? No one in a *right mind* would dare. People or nation-states who are not of a *right mind*, who may even have legitimate complaints about economic sanctions or American policies, can only receive adequate redress when they give in to playing the economic game by the international rules that has been developed and brokered by the United States of America, which insures American dominance and hegemony. We are very lucky to be Americans, because it's always much better to be on the winning side than anywhere else. And as citizens, we have much we collectively owe to the brave soldiers who have fought on foreign battlefields, to prevent our homeland from becoming a future battlefield. Despite all of our faults as a culture, our imperfect government and legal system, and criticisms regarding our over consumptive superficial lifestyles, America remains the most powerful nation in the history of planet Earth.

America continues to set high standards for all people who believe in freedom, justice, and equal opportunity. The Homeland Security Act was quickly enacted to protect us, and while some civil liberties have been cut back, American is still by far the "land of the free, and the home of the brave." It's far better to be relatively free and alive, than to be anarchically free, and dead. We all must make our temporary sacrifices, and until the world is relatively safe again for the citizens of our planet, we should trust our government to do the best job that they can for us. Fighting an invisible enemy cannot possibly be an easy job.

American power comes from the fact that the world owes the US so much, most of which is still outstanding debt, and the fact that real patriots love our nation so much that they are willing to put their lives in harms way, time and time again. Those nations who are stupid enough to bite the hand that feeds them (like several countries our military has helped to free in the past), and then they will not receive an invitation to dine. Or there can be long-lasting peace among the neighborhoods, as long as interests aren't threatened, and Americans are safe to travel to any neighborhood in the world.

I thank God that I was not born a Taliban, and that I enjoy all the blessings and opportunities we have in America... it's at least 1000 times better than living in Afghanistan. And while I admire the two female missionaries for their devotion to their Christian beliefs, they must realize that most Islamic regimes are not anywhere close to being tolerant of religion, as guaranteed by our Constitution. In fact, many Islamic states follow the Nazi philosophy of rounding up people who don't believe like them, then subjecting them to kangaroo trials, then executing them. American soldiers risked their lives to protect Christians from intolerance by saving our American missionaries from the Taliban.

We should not accept the legitimacy of any regime that executes innocent people solely on account of their personal religious beliefs. Any nation, whether Islamic or whatever who practices religious fascism, and have such anti-Christian laws and customs, should not benefit from trade or protection, because one of the primary founding principles of this land, America, was religious freedom. America is the world's torch holder of religious freedom, and here, we don't arrest Moslems
and execute them on account of their belief in Islam... we do so only if they are terrorists. Here in America, people from all world religions can live side by side in peace, without government persecution or harassment (a few nuts may be guilty, but not our laws, government, and culture). God bless America and our countless unsung heroes from shore to shore, and all who risk their lives daily on foreign soil so we may remain prosperous and free to worship who we want.

Letter to the CIA Director circa 2003:

Dear Director George Tenet,

Salutations, and best wishes for a safe and Happy New Year to you all our American patriots at the CIA. Americans should be thankful for the heroic efforts of CIA agents to combat our enemies abroad, and those in our homeland who conspire with our foes. America should also be thankful for your personal patriotism, honesty and loyalty to the great principles that form the foundation of American democracy. Under your leadership, America is fighting off attacks from both "supposed friends" and foes alike. The CIA remains the last true uncorrupted bastion of government remaining that is protecting the United States from international and domestic conspirators who desire to see America fall to its knees, in order for them to gain power, prestige and wealth.

I am writing to you to describe what I've recognized as an evolving agenda to disrupt, manipulate and control the economy and government of the United States of America. The news media and university systems have done a great disservice to the CIA and our nation since the Vietnam War by negatively portraying the CIA. Who stands to gain from efforts to take over control of the CIA?

1. Corrupt politicians who owe their allegiances to special interest groups who are funded or bribed by America's competitors, foes, foreign governments, criminal enterprises, and rouge despots. They desire to limit the CIA's ability to gather damaging data, intelligence and evidence of their conspiracies and disloyalty to America.

2. Criminal organizations who want to destroy the CIA's ability to track down their criminal activities, crime networks and high connections to executives in the banking, investments, insurance and political networks. We need not look very far to discover a pattern of entanglement between financiers and traffickers in the domestic and international drug trade, which generates funds for illegal arms trading that provides terrorists with their caches.

3. Corrupt bureaucrats who have been enticed by slick, dishonest, and tricky investment brokers and bankers to squander public funds on ridiculous and highly risky investment scams.

How can local and state government treasurers live lifestyles that should exceed the means of their salaries? The Orange County fiasco with Merrill Lynch (part of the Chicago-based elite bankers and criminal network that is the hub of much drug and terrorist funds), and the California budget deficit are "smoking guns" as records should prove our local governments have been swindled. How many bureaucrats have access to secret offshore numbered accounts that were set up to hide kickbacks or paybacks?

Director Tenet, I understand that you are of Greek heritage, and we all know how the Greeks were the greatest and most advanced democratic and technological civilization of their time. Yet, the great Greek civilization eventually fell, and history has clearly delineated the causes of its decline. Is America, the greatest and most advanced democratic and technological civilization of recent times vulnerable to similar patterns that led to the fall of the great Greek empire? I'm concerned that there are concerted secretive alliances that form an international conspiracy that is attempting to control strategic segments of American society, government, economy, education system, media, and laws.

There is ample evidence, based on public records and news reports that point to specific groups and their conspiratorial networks that are working 24/7 to undermine destabilize and manipulate the American system to their own advantage and benefit. Where are the hubs of this geo-political conspiracy? We need not look very far.

1. The main group at the center of this unpatriotic hub lies in the city of Chicago, and then connects to Las Vegas, New York city (including Boston and New Jersey), and to a lesser extent to San Francisco and Los Angeles. These networks of high financiers provide the funds for illegal activities, which they see as just another avenue to high and often illegal profits. This network has access to criminal organizations that provides the foot soldiers and infrastructure required to move drugs, illegal arms, and other illegal activities. This same group of financiers then use their banks and firms to launder money from illegally gotten gains from criminal organizations, as they collect their commissions for sanitizing the finances of the crime syndicates.

2. The players in this expansive clandestine network includes very legitimate names in banking, commodities and mercantile exchanges, investment banking, stock brokerages, corporate CEO's and CFO's, accounting and auditing firms, politicians at all levels, corrupt local law enforcement officials,

bureaucrats, foreign spies (including those of our supposed allies), military contractors and subcontractors, and special interest lobbyist (many who are actually foreign spies). Cooperating with this group of financiers and gatekeepers are the crime syndicates, drug cartels, and various terrorist groups. These networks form an underground network of high finances that is hidden from the federal government, regulatory agencies, the Department of Treasury, the I.R.S., and the F.B.I.

3. The types of illegal investments and activities include:

a. Money laundering, off shore tax havens, and secret bank accounts used to clean and hide "dirty money."

b. Drug trafficking, financing, and corporate fronts.

c. Illegal arms trade to rouge states and terrorists.

d. Corruption of key officials in our government, agencies, law enforcement, corporations and political parties.

e. Stock market and commodities price manipulations, insider trading and other illegal trading practices, bribes, kickbacks, embezzlement, falsification of accounting records, tax evasion, and other financial crimes.

f. Use of hedge funds and capital from wealthy individuals to invest in various schemes to short stocks and to attack monetary values, to crash stock markets and to cause hyper-inflation if it serves to turn a quick profit.

g. Multi-national corporations (MNCs) that do substantial business or receive investment or accounting consultation from members of this clandestine high finance network can provide logistical support for spies to access American technology at the point of production. For example, if a foreign government wants to obtain secrets to America's F-35 JSA - Joint Strike Fighter, MNCs and their subsidiaries can act to transfer technology from military contracts to the "go-between" spies, who then sell it or give it to our enemies and competitors. The international connection through international bankers, deal brokers, military procurement board, and foreign governments should be closely monitored.

In the past decade, it has been through this elaborate conspiracy network that Bin Laden become party to selling Afghan/Taliban heroin to the Columbian and Mexican drug cartels, whose money was then laundered by banks, investment brokerages and corporations, who invested drug deals. When Bin Laden's $500 million drug shipment was seized in April 2001, he needed to recoup his losses. The Elite bankers in Chicago likely loaned him funds to short the stock market, then he attacked the World Trade Center to drive down stock prices; thereby making a profit to recoup his initial drug losses and to repay the Elite bankers for their initial investment in his drugs. It was the Bin Laden's intent to convert drug monies into arms and WMDs that included purchasing brief case nukes from the Chechens, which he then would have sleeper cells plant in various cities across the United States. He would then simultaneously detonate all such implanted nukes by having one of his lieutenants call from a prepaid cell phone to trigger the WMDs. One of the "modus operandi" of Bin Laden is to execute well-planned multi-prong large attacks that could kill large numbers of innocent people, while driving a spike into the heart of the American economy.

Al-Qaeda is but one strategy to attempt to weaken Americans and the government, culture, and way of life. The long-range goal of various anti-American conspirators is simple, and we are witnessing the results of its insidious plot as our society continues to decay in all areas.

1. Social decay through propagating disunity among Americans.

a. Fuel racism by blaming whites for all of society's ills, thus driving a wedge between minority races and the majority.

b. Promote immorality and divisive cultural-ethnic-racial-sex conflicts by legalizing homosexual marriages, pornography, illegal immigration, affirmative action, late term abortion, and encouraging degeneration through mass media.

c. Promote interracial conflict by creating ineffective minority hand out programs that pits one race against another.

d. Create disrespect for authority and government by slowly outlawing basic freedoms, and creating too much red tape.

e. Cause ethical and moral decay by outlawing reasonable corporal punishment of children for destructive conduct, where a reasonable degree of punishment by parents and teachers would otherwise keep certain students from lives of crime. Instead, disrespectful children become rebellious teens who eventually spend most of their lives as adults in prison, becoming subjected to highly violent environments that far exceed the penalty of a loving spanking when it could have made a positive difference in their young lives.

f. Suppress and ridicule good citizenship and patriotism, while promoting sex, violence, and greed as the "cool" and desirable lifestyle.

g. Resist progressive changes to the education system, such as school vouchers. Mix all children into template classes, so disinterested and disruptive children ruin the learning environment for students who wish to learn. Penalize the teachers by making them suspect for every frivolous and false accusation from dysfunctional students.

2. Political decay by media and universities encouraging distrust of government, particularly the federal government.

a. Special interest groups and political lobbyists entice and corrupt government officials, politicians, and bureaucrats.

b. Alienate citizens from governance by making them feel disinterested and hopeless to positively change policies. When citizens no longer monitor government activities, there is greater latitude for corruptive influences to make significant inroads.

c. Persuade corrupted legislators and agency chiefs to make policies that favor special interest groups, while punishing citizens, thereby transferring citizens' money to Elites.

3. Economic decay is evidenced by a strategy of wealth transfer from the working middle class to special interests Elites.

a. The US is treated as just another consumer market for exploitation and wealth building by the Elites, thus the ends justify the means, and patriotism is not a concern.

b. Swindle retirees of their life savings and pensions through clever investment ruses and fraud. Past Enron, Arthur Andersen and Merrill Lynch corruption is only the tip of the iceberg. Law enforcement must identify (use reverse phone tree) and round up the top executives from this conspiratorial network to prevent them from corrupting every person and corporation that they touch and bribe; otherwise, they and those like them will breed like cockroaches, and soon it will be near impossible to exterminate them.

c. Use technology to replace American workers, to maximize corporate profits and CEO compensation under the guise of necessity and competitive survivability, instead of their true motive of wanton greed.

d. Outsource manufacturing and white-collar high tech jobs to cheap labor markets, even if the consequence is harmful to the US economy.

e. Concentrate control of strategic industries, raw materials, and consumer markets to MNCs whose executives have no loyalty to America, but only to wealth building.

f. Destabilize the US dollar to cause sudden and massive monetary devaluations, and de-dollarize international trade when the monetary and trade imbalances makes currencies ripe for hedge fund speculation and attacks.

4. International relations decay by attempting to discredit, isolate and alienate President Bush and our government on the world stage.

a. Implement anti-Bush and anti-American propaganda tactics.

b. Use Elite-controlled domestic and international news media to foment anti-American sentiments through biased news editing, reporting, and commentary represented as factual.

c. Foment violence, conflicts and insurgency to test American diplomatic and military response, and to stretch out America's resources abroad, thereby weakening the frontlines.

d. Criticize response as being either too little too late, too heavy-handed and unilateralist, or too insensitive, or whatever slant is necessary to discredit America's good deeds abroad.

e. Foster anti-American sentiments to unify different political and religious camps by recognizing the USA as their common foe, by applying the "Your enemy's enemy is your friend" principle. This strategy is being used among Islamic states, anti-Semitic groups, and terrorist networks. A unified Europe, Sino-Russian rapprochement, and unified South America all present potential hot spots in fomenting future anti-American sentiments.

5. Military decay through compromise, spying, and overextension.

   a. Dependency on foreign manufacturers, suppliers, and raw materials needed for military hardware and systems

   b. Spies and moles planted in sensitive government agencies and committees with oversight over intelligence, military technology, procurement, and operations.

c. Government contracts and subcontracts that allow foreign corporations (thus governments) to monitor our military and government communication through service providers of email, phone, fax, computer hardware and software.

d. Installation of "back door" chips or spy software in military and government computer networks and equipment, such as computers, planes, trucks, offices, and ships for spying.

e. Integration of "override" chips or software programs into military weapons and communications systems to permit partial or complete take over, sabotage, or destruction of vulnerable military systems, such as virtual battlefield and
the Joint Strike Fighter.

f. Install spy technology into sensitive American facilities, buildings, vehicles, and offices through construction, art work, furniture, equipment, housekeeping and security contractors and suppliers.

I also have immediate concern for the safety of the entire Bush family, as Bin Laden has shown his determination to finish jobs, where he had failed on a previous attempt. All of the Bush's residences must be adequately controlled by effective security measures to prevent car or truck bombs, which are the preferred choice of attack by suicidal terrorists. Since security around President Bush is likely tightened, the rest of the Bush family would make more "opportune targets", and as all terrorists and criminals know, they can really hurt someone badly by targeting the families of their targets. Please ask President Bush to have the Secret Service and Homeland Security improve security measures for the entire Bush family, especially for his parents and his lovely daughters.

With the advent of this new millennium, we entered into a new global paradigm, where interrelationships between bankers and stockbrokers become intermingled with the mutual monetary goals of drug cartels, illegal arms merchants, enemy states, corrupt politicians, criminal syndicates, and international terrorists. The flow of drugs and weapons is often financed by diverting legitimate funds, with illegal profits washed clean through money-laundering networks abetted by domestic and international banks. It has become difficult to track down the financiers of terrorism only because on the surface, they appear to be legitimate individuals, above suspicion, but occupying high perches from which great financial benefits are derived.

I hope you and the CIA will be successful in tracking down all those greedy and unscrupulous high financiers (some whom are Elite) who have no patriotism and no qualms about secretly making deals that eventually support terrorist networks who seek to kill innocent people, disrupt democratic economies, and to cause public sentiment to depose the great defenders of our liberties, such as President George W. Bush and Prime Minister Tony Blair.

In the following pages, I present descriptions of various inventions and strategies that our military must undertake to insure that American wins this war in Iraq, and the war on terrorism. I'd be honored to clarify these and other concepts to help our government to defeat the forces of evil. After "911", I sent emails to our senators, news media, FBI, and to President Bush at the Whitehouse detailing what I called "Terrorist Targeting Tactics", and asked our Senators to support the "Bush Doctrine" of pre-emptive engagement against Saddam Hussein, once diplomatic efforts had failed in the U.N. I don't know if my ideas were ever read or considered, by I was glad to see our government take appropriate steps similar to that presented.

I, like a majority of Americans support President Bush's effort to protect our homeland from attacks, even though we suspect no system is perfect, and at times terrorists will be somewhat successful in creating death, destruction, and mayhem. President George W. Bush is the first American president to place our nation on a "proactive" footing, rather than to wait to be attacked by our enemies first, then reacting after the fact. The old adage, "an ounce of prevention is worth a pound of cure" is still very appropriate to our new post-modern high tech era. The following describes concepts of military weapons that must be developed to insure America's security in this hostile and unpredictable new world of terrorism.

1. Break-away engine shrouds should be designed to break off from aircraft once hit by a heat-seeking surface to air missile (SAM). The engine shroud should be made of a heat retentive material that makes it, and not the aircraft's engines, the hottest "heat signature" to attract a SAM's heat-seeking guidance targeting system. When a SAM hits this engine shroud, it is jettisoned along with exploding debris caused by the SAM, and thus in most cases, sparing the aircraft's vital engine assembly.

2. Armored ATV's and scooters are a cheaper and more effective alternative to HumV's, and offers superior protection to "foot patrols" which have become standing targets in Iraq's urban duck shoot. This class of vehicles is easy to maneuver, can access tight and narrow streets, and chase insurgents right into their hideouts, where HumV's and other large vehicles could not. Mount machine guns, RPG's and rockets to these off-road, all-terrain vehicles, and the terrorist insurgents won't have a chance to run and hide. Our troops would be quick and deadly!

3. Shock-absorbing concrete barriers should be built to dissipate blast effect though water or gel chambers. These barriers must be of varying heights, as appropriate to protect roads, military facilities, and taller civilian buildings.

4. A coordinated troop security strategy must be implemented.

a. Helicopters must not fly in tight formations, but staggered and set at least 100 yards apart to prevent easy targeting, or in the event one is hit, careening into other helicopters.

b. American and coalition troops need to stop walking blindly into ambushes. No more routine foot patrols to draw enemy fire and RPGs. Troops should be the "SWAT" to back up Iraqi police, and not be first response teams.

c. Certain main road arteries must be fortified and restricted to coalition force travel only, with routine mine sweeping before convoys travel the routes.

d. Buildings and facilities security must be coordinated, with cameras, deep ditches, blast-dampening concrete barriers, sunken and reinforced metal poles, and other measures to detect terrorists to prevent them from entering the "green zone" of any protected facility.

e. Gunshot, RPG, grenade, and rocket-launching detection position triangulation technology (similar to that used by the LAPD) must be utilize to quickly locate the positions from which insurgents are launching their attacks.

f. Robot mine detection vehicles (similar to remote controlled toy cars) must precede any troop patrols or convoys. We must be able to detect, and then explode ordinances before they are activated as our convoys and troops pass by.

g. Laser border detection equipment should be developed and employed at least 1000 yards from secured facilities to detect insurgents; to prevent them from reaching a deadly range to launch mortars, grenades, or small arms attacks.

5. Killer satellites are a must, especially now that communist China has joined the space race, and we can't totally rely on friendly future relations between America and nations who are capable of deploying nuclear weapons against us. Worse case scenarios must be developed to anticipate any future potential threat from China, No. Korea, Russia, India, Pakistan,

Chechnya, or other states with real or potential sizable anti-American sentiments among the majority of its population or in its governments.

6. The NMD, national missile defense system is a must. I have included a concept for an effective missile shield that coordinates GPS telemetry with the deployment of a debris field ahead of incoming missiles. A debris field is dispersed by an anti-ballistic missile ahead of the incoming missile's trajectory, then continues to engage it's target with a high explosive warhead. Should the defensive missile miss its target, the target missile will then enter into the debris field of explosive mini-mines that was left ejected by the engaging defensive missile. The hostile incoming missile is thus destroyed when it collides with the debris field, as all mini-mines automatically and simultaneously explodes when the hostile missile collides with any one of them. This maximizes the blast effect, while eliminating the possible mining of earth orbit and space, which would make space travel and satellite survival more dangerous for all nations, including America.
7. A supersonic attack helicopter will greatly enhance our military flexibility and arsenal, where Harrier-type "jump" jets might not be effective. The concept should use a hybrid design between propeller and jet engines, and a shielded stealth airfoil.

8. Spies and moles must be rooted out from the civilian agencies, bureaucracy and military contractors and subs that deal with weapons design, development, and production. If we continue to outsource the building of our military weapons systems, the military will lose control of its own military machine. For example, if we allow our military contractors to sub-contract the electronics, guidance, and weapons targeting systems to Israel (as an example), it would be possible for them to design various "backdoors" into our weapons systems, to permit them or their proxies to seize control of our weapons deployed in a battlefield.
9. The Joint Strike Fighter program, slated to be battle ready by 2008, must be safeguarded. This system reportedly allows generals to coordinate and control real time battles from a distant command center, let's say, from NORAD or Pentagon. These advanced jet fighter/bombers can be controlled remotely, and in theory can be flown without pilots (they can perform maneuvers that could kill human pilots by excessive "g" forces). Imagine companies who install the virtual battlefield equipment, computers, and software could secretly insert override points, which would allow them access and total control over the system, then turn our own advanced nuclear capable weapons on us! Unlikely? Not if we outsource our technology, then rely on foreigners to build our weapons systems.

This has already happened. Just ask Senator McCain why he has proposed an immediate cessation to outsourcing policies initiated by our greedy Pentagon civilian procurement board that had previously locked our military contractors to subcontract with Israel for key communication and electronics work on our most secret military weapons systems, and how they stole our technology to build the most advanced tanks and surface to air missiles in the world. I hope it's not too late for us. Build American and safeguard our homeland now and for generations to come.

10. Greater support, funding, and upgrading of the CIA's ability and equipment to gather accurate intelligence on our potential foes, supposed allies (Israel, German, France, China, and Russia), and our true enemies (terrorists states who support terrorists).

Our homeland and military are exposed to many areas of vulnerability, and I have mentioned just the "tip of the iceberg." Mega-greed knows no loyalty to nation, culture, ideals, or people. Greedy people are hypocrites, serpents, and a brood of vipers. To those who worship money, the ends justify the means, and they are fully capable of employing any means necessary to achieve their greedy financial goals. Terrorism, drug dealing, illegal arms trade, mega-corporate mergers, political corruption and investment scams are just the tools that are employed to derive their ill gotten wealth. A house divided cannot stand long; consequently the multi-pronged attacks against fundamental American institutions continue to go unabated, and except for the courageous efforts of the CIA and other key agencies, our enemies can weaken us by monitoring or controlling key communication and administration hubs that compromise our military, political, economic, social, and international relations institutions and personnel. Our enemies have a common agenda to bring America down.

How can the CIA rise to the occasion to neutralize our enemies and so-called self-benefiting and disloyal friends, who continue to attack and spy on America? It's a big job, and it won't be easy, but no other agency has the loyalty, guts, resources, talent, and ability to fight the fight. Only the CIA can save America, because you are an honest and patriotic public servant who commands a group of highly trained, patriotic, and loyal people.

Globalization and the rapid rise of MNCs, elitist CEO's and oligarchs signal the rapid demise of ethics, morality, patriotism, and humanitarianism. We need not look too far to the event horizon to see our potential futures destroyed by international carpetbaggers and terrorists. We must win a secret war on the secret financiers of global terror soon, otherwise it will be too late for us and our children's generation.

Please accept my sincere thanks, gratitude, and appreciation for taking your time to review and consider vital aspects of this communication. May God shine his grace and blessings upon you, your family, and the CIA.

Sincerely,

A patriot and loyal911american
philamerican2004@yahoo.com

May God Bless America...

I hope our government will be able to prevent the next levels of terrorism...

1. Cyber sabotage of infrastructure
2. Biological & viral infestation
3. Nuclear detonations
4. Genetic genocide

All can be done without the presence of suicidal human conspirators... an "plain" package aboard a ship or plane, then a cell phone call detonation.

Force as a response may feel good, but will it then escalate terrorism to a worse level? What are the root causes that must be resolved to prevent more of these types of atrocities? Can we really find the guilty parties and bring them to justice without making them martyrs to their twisted causes? Are these violent episodes indicative of human nature, a history filled with violence, war, and genocide?

We all grieve, as a nation, as people, as Americans. I pray for all the souls given up in the struggle of Good against evil, and for their families and loved ones. I hope America and the free world will win.

FBI/CIA WARNS OF FURTHER TERRORISTS ATTACKS

But they obviously don't know where, when, and by whom.

A lot of good that does, except to make people more afraid, keeping people away from large crowds, and having negative economic consequences on the national economy (except for "at home" type activities, maybe we'll buy more televisions, short-wave radios, cell phones, emergency water and ratios, computers, guns, and gas masks... make more babies?).

So here's my best guess based on what little we know about how terrorists, and Osama bin Laden types misbehave:

1. They strike at symbols of American strength to show our weaknesses (to disrespectfully spit in our face).

2. They strike at highly populated venues to maximize destruction, death and carnage, more bang for the buck (or suicidal crazy asshole).

3. They go after physically large objects (they must all be near-sighted son's of bitches).

4. They strike around some symbolic dates or numbers known to American pop culture or related to support of Israel (9-11, Halloween, Thanksgiving, Christmas, Easter, July 4th, etc. What's next? Boo!).

5. Their intent is to create massive fear among the population, to "castrate" our manhood, to make us like bitches hiding out in our homes instead of at the nightclubs or jobs (reflects their twisted oppressive attitudes toward women, including our Lady Liberty).

6. They don't want Americans to have fun or enjoy our lives because they are miserable sons of bitches, living in the middle of nowhere, with no showers. They know they can count our news media to do their propaganda work for them, by spreading fear.

7. Conclusion: I have no proof, but my best guess is Las Vegas, on Halloween or likely Thanksgiving weekend (has national historical significance), spreading toxic chemicals upwind from the strip, unless they can hijack a jet from McCarran Field, the commercial airport in Las Vegas. Or they'll go into a restrooms, change clothes, re-emerge in National Guard fatigues, take bombs or weapons hidden by accomplices disguised as janitors, AND

8. Screw that. I'm going to Vegas anyway (but I'll probably take along my gas mask in addition to water). And I don't plan to stay at the Strato-sphere, or that big gold looking hotel, and for sure not at the New York, New York. Hey, if they're not too angry at the Egyptians, the Luxor might be okay. Life is a gamble, isn't it? Yep.

Financiers of Terrorism

Our government is concentrating its effort to protect the United States homeland from international and domestic conspirators who desire to see America fall to its knees, in order for them to gain domestic and international power, prestige and wealth in the rapidly evolving globalized world order. Our enemies have a common agenda to disrupt, manipulate and control the economy and government of the United States of America through various covert and disguised strategies, which include networks of:

1. Corrupt politicians who owe their allegiances to special interest groups and their political lobbyists who are funded or bribed by America's foes, competitors, foreign governments, criminal enterprises, and rouge despots. They directly, indirectly, or inadvertently assist foreign interests to gather and cover up damaging data, intelligence and evidence of their conspiracies and disloyalty to the United States of America.
2. Criminal organizations who want to destroy our government's ability to track down their criminal activities, crime networks and high level social and financial connections to executives in the banking, investments, monetary funds, insurance and political networks. We need not look very far to discover a pattern of entanglement between financiers and traffickers in the domestic and international drug trade that generates funds for illegal arms trading, which provide terrorists with their caches and WMD's.
3. Corrupt bureaucrats who have been enticed by slick, dishonest, and tricky investment brokers and bankers to squander public funds on ridiculous and highly risky investment scams. How can local and state government treasurers live lifestyles that should

exceed the means of their salaries? The Orange County fiasco with Merrill Lynch, and the California budget deficit are smoking guns as records should prove our local governments have been swindled. How many corrupt bureaucrats and corporate executives have access to secret offshore numbered accounts that were set up to hide kickbacks or paybacks, and to avoid paying federal taxes? We need to investigate and discover the facts. The Chicago-based Elite bankers and organized crime network is likely the hub of drug and terrorist funding, and corruption of government and executives.

The Greeks were the greatest and most advanced democratic and technological civilization or their time. Yet, the great Greek civilization eventually fell, and history has clearly delineated the causes of its decline.

Is America, the greatest and most advanced democratic and technological civilization of recent times vulnerable to similar patterns that led to the fall of the great Greek empire? Secretive alliances that form an international conspiracy is attempting to greatly influence or control strategic segments of American society, government, economy, education system, media, and laws. They are also trying to compromise our military command.

The types of illegal investments and activities include:

a. Money laundering, off shore tax havens, and secret bank accounts used to clean and hide "dirty money."
b. Drug trafficking, financing, and corporate fronts.
c. Illegal arms trade to rouge states and terrorists.
d. Corruption of key officials in our government,

agencies, law enforcement, corporations and political parties.

e. Stock market and commodities price manipulation, insider trading and other illegal trading practices, bribes, kickbacks,
embezzlement, falsification of accounting records, tax evasion, and other financial crimes.

f. Use of hedge funds and capital from wealthy individuals to invest in various schemes to short stocks and to attack monetary values, to crash stock markets and to cause hyperinflation if it serves to turn a quick and huge profit, even if that causes nations to become bankrupt, including future attacks against the U.S. Dollar and U.K. Pound.

g. Multi-national corporations: MNCs that do substantial business or receive investment or accounts consultation from members of this clandestine high finance network provide logistical
support for spies to access American technology at the point of production. For example, if a foreign government wants to obtain secrets to America's Joint Strike Fighter, MNCs and their subsidiaries can transfer technology from military sub-contracts to the "go-between" spies, who then sell it or give it to our enemies and competitors.

The Elite bankers, dealmakers, brokers, the military procurement board, and certain governments should be closely monitored. In the past decade, it's been through this elaborate conspiracy network that bin Laden become party to selling Afghan/Taliban heroin to the Columbian and Mexican drug cartels, with distribution through various crime families. Banks, investment brokerages and corporations who invested in drug deals with the help of domestic crime organizations then laundered drug money profits. When bin Laden's $500 million drug shipment was seized in April 2001, he needed to recoup his losses. Elite bankers in Chicago likely loaned him funds to short the stock market, then he attacked the World Trade Center to drive down stock prices; thereby making a profit to recoup his initial drug losses and to repay Elite bankers for their initial investment in his drugs.

It was the bin Laden's intent to convert drug monies into arms and WMDs that included purchasing brief case nukes from the Chechens, which he then could have sleeper cells plant in various cities across the United States. He could then simultaneously detonate all such implanted nukes by having one of his lieutenants call from a prepaid or stolen cell phone to trigger the WMDs. One of the "modus operandi" of bin Laden is to execute well-planned multi-prong large attacks that could kill large numbers of innocent people, while driving a spike into the heart of the American economy. What's he up to next? Let's hope the U.S. will be able to sniff his plans out before he has the capability to execute another of his dastardly attacks, as he has boasted, this time that will destroy an American city.

Chapter 3 – The Tactics

The 3 T's: Terrorist Targeting Tactics

It is almost impossible to put oneself in the mindset of suicidal terrorists; but failure to do so leaves our nation, people, and way of life vulnerable to terrorist attacks. Following are some potential ways terrorists can select their targets, and the reason why, and how to fight it. We must recognize that terrorists want to cause the greatest amount of destruction, loss of life, civil unrest, lost of national confidence, and economic collapse in our American civilization. Terrorists also attempt to maximize "bang for the buck," and consequently attempt to do the most damage with the least costly method, often resorting to relatively low-tech strategies. If we can prevent the "biggies" from happening, terrorists are left with Palestinian-type atrocities, which would affect less people, and not cause as much disruption to our economy.

Potential Targets: ***Likely Methods and why:***

1. **Gas station underground.** Time delay device dropped into underground storage tanks through fill caps of the tanks, or if buying gasoline, run bomb laden suicidal vehicle into pumps. resulting in public paranoia, affecting prices to hurt economy.

2. **Gas tanker trucks.** Shoot them up and grenade launchers in rush hour traffic launchers from vehicles to build paranoia in public and to raise transport costs.

3. **Large School Bldgs.** Shoot up the kids, or wire buildings for detonation to cause fear in parents for children's safety.

4. **Nuclear Power Plants.** Explode large fertilizer truck bombs in parking lots next to nuclear plants to cause massive radioactive release, deaths and illnesses.

5. **Nuke Major Cities.** Briefcase nukes onboard commercial jets, ships, vehicles, or hidden in buildings or public lockers, and mini-storage facilities, etc. to cause massive chaos, disruption, fear, and panic to collapse economy.

6. **Major bridges**. Cause a major blockage at both ends, and then blow it up during high commuting periods to cause fear of bridges.

7. **Major ports.** Tactical nuke onboard cargo container with remote trigger, same as nuking cities to ruin ship economy.

8. **Major airports.** "Dirty nukes" that disperse radioactive waste contained in baggage to create major kill zones.

9. **Commercial jets.** Shoot portable SAMs or RPGs at jets on low altitude landing approach to create fear of flying.

10. **Major rail stations.** Biochemical/biological or detonate briefcase nuke to create major kill zone (MKZ).

11. **Major bus terminals.** Same as rail station MKZ.

12. **Churches & synagogues.** Wire and blow up buildings to strike at non-Islamic religions.

13. **Water Aqueducts.** Bacteriological contamination to cause massive deaths.

14. **Major dams.** Blow up with TNT for massive deaths.

15. **Power grid towers.** Blow up key links in tower for blackouts.

16. **Woodland homes.** Start many fires during dry summers to cause major damage, destruction and deaths.

17. **Forests.** Start fires all over to drain response resources.

18. **Lakes.** Dump toxic chemicals or bio toxins to cause mass deaths.

19. **Airborne.** Bacterial and viral release to cause mass illness.

20. **Human contact.** Bacterial or viral hosts to infect population.

21. **Large Apartment complexes.** Wire with explosives and blow up to cause deaths and fear.

22. **Large office buildings.** Van bombs in parking structures to cause massive deaths or put bio/chemical agents in central AC.

23. **Indoor shopping malls.** Suicidal bomb squads to cause massive deaths and fear.

Targets/Method: *Solutions:*

1. Bombing gas stations. Fill caps must be locked, with double redundancy, no universal tanker driver keys.

2. Shooting gas tankers. Gasoline tankers restricted from freeways during rush hour, and must make deliveries during non-busy periods.

3. Shoot up/bomb schools. Night scope cameras installed at all schools, with central office monitoring to detect unauthorized personnel at sites, backed up by periodic sweeps by bomb sniffing dogs.

4. Bomb nuclear plants. Build blast walls around nuclear reactors; restrict adjacent areas only to small vehicles, with road barriers and deep ditches, etc.

5. Nuke major cities. Radiation detectors at all major highways, ports, airports, & borders. Fast response teams to take out terrorists who plant nukes. Control borders (computer chip all INS detainees and deportees). High reliability informants, spies, infiltrators, and double agents. Bribe the Russian mob & KGB from arming terrorists, so they sell to our CIA agents, set up the terrorists, and get double the ante. If terrorists are willing to pay $200 million,

we offer $400 million. Then we work with nuclear governments to plug the nuclear theft gaps.

6. Major bridges. Night scope and infrared cameras and automated bomb sniffing sensors, daily bomb sniffing dog inspection, and visual inspections.

7. Major ports. Radiation detectors for all incoming cargo, while ships are 100 mi. off the US coastline, to be cleared by Coast Guard before entry.

8. Major airports. Radiation detectors at international airports for all inbound planes (especially freight), before jets are allowed to park at terminals. Radiation detectors at all major domestic airports. Equip jets with special radar and automatic countermeasures against missiles.

9. Commercial jets. Anti-missile counter measures.

10. Major rail stations. Biochemical and biological toxin detectors. Air supply checked by automatic sensors around the clock. Radiation sensors at every station.

11. Major bus terminals. Same as rail stations.

12. Churches/synagogues. Same as schools' strategy.

13. California Aqueduct. Bacteria and chemical toxin testing and monitoring continuously.

14. Major dams. Cameras, and expanded secured no trespass zones.

15. Power grid towers. Plane and jeep patrols of remote but key towers in the regional and national transmission grids, with night scope cameras. Real time security camera system linking up all transmission towers.

16. Woodland homes. More emphasis and patrol by local law enforcement of potential hazard areas, greater citizen watch, and major brush clearances.

17. Forests. Increase number of rangers and fire equipment. Improve air and ground response times, and access roads. More smoke spotting personnel, better camp fire safety enforcement activities.

18. Lakes. Increased testing and monitoring for chemical or bacterial agents, with rapid closure, evacuation, and triage after exposure.

19. Airborne. Better security at small craft airports and rural airports.

20. Human contact. Quicker response time and coordination with CDC, hospitals, etc. Total quarantine, all schools and businesses to lock down, people to remain in homes, until deadly virus transmission is controlled.

21. Large Apartment complexes. Better screening of tenants, and managers to improve apartment watch and tenant relations programs.

22. Large office buildings. Regular patrol of sensitive areas of internal parking structures, with faster evacuation and emergency response, use of temporary steel girders to reinforce foundation and building frame. Camera monitor and security access only to AC unit and service areas, but doesn't solve problem of recirculating air from within units, except must exhaust all building air, instead of recirculation.

22. Indoor shopping malls. "Face print" linkage to FBI database in real time to spot terrorists. Improved border control to keep out known terrorists.

These are but a few of potential terrorist targets, and our nation is rich in assets, any of which could become targeted by determined terrorists and their supporters. Unless Bin Laden and his top aides are caught or killed soon, it is likely that they will try to carry through with their threats to explode nukes in American cities. All we can do is pray that our intelligence network and military will get to al-Qaeda before they can strike at us again. Let's hope Congress gives the Homeland Security Department, the CIA, and FBI all the funds they need.

To: Governor Tom Ridge, Director of Homeland Security

cc: FBI, CIA, and Law Enforcement Community

Subject: The Three "Ts" = Terrorist Targeting Tactics

Is the al-Qaeda information about the next terrorist attack on American soil based on misinformation from prisoners who are liars? If "truth serum" and torture is not being used to obtain accurate data from al-Qaeda terrorists, then we should suspect the authenticity of their claims and plots.

Is it possible that the announced potential terrorist plots to blow up apartment buildings may be a diversion or decoy from other dastardly plans? Let's analyze the 3T's...

Terrorist Objectives:

1. Create maximum terror
2. Cause maximum economic disruption
3. Obtain maximum "bang for the buck"
4. Attack large targets to maximize death and destruction
5. Use unusual and unexpected attack methods
6. When possible, attack around days symbolic to the

Discussion:

1. Creating maximum terror is accomplished by using the mass media to plant fear of uncertainty, by creating a sensationalistic environment of speculation.

2. Causing maximum economic disruption is achieved by attacking institutions, systems, and organizations that directly impact our national economic health because it attacks our self-confidence and trust in our system of life.

3. Obtaining maximum "bang for the buck" is to use low cost and relatively low-tech methods to build and deliver weapons of mass destruction by utilizing "normalcy" in unthinkable and abnormal ways, beyond rational thought.

4. Attack large targets to maximize death and destruction. Killing a few hundred people in a theater or nightclub is the strategy of Palestinian suicide bombers. Murdering possibly tens or hundreds of thousands of innocent civilians is the strategy of al-Qaeda.

5. Use unusual or unexpected attack methods to minimize discovery, and to maximize surprise and unpreparedness. Often, movie scenarios or news stories are used because
it exposes likely vulnerabilities that already exist, and which most people don't believe could happen again, or are fictional, thus are not likely to happen.

6. Attack around days that are symbolic to America's cultural or political culture and psychology... to "mind fuck" us, and thus to make maximum propaganda and psychological warfare advances.

Without causing undue public alarm, as a precaution, the law enforcement community should walk their bomb-sniffing dogs around large high school buildings that house 2000-3000 students. Incidents where students at Columbine, San Diego, and Germany have succeeded to inflict death and mayhem, and they were only deranged untrained kids, not professional killers like al-Qaeda.

An opportune time for the two-dozen alleged terrorists, who may have sneaked into the port of NYC onboard cargo containers, is over holiday weekends, such as Memorial Day or July 4th activities and celebrations. If crowded venues, shopping malls, rail, bridges are not attacked, then perhaps they could rig up large vacant high school buildings for detonation, when filled again with innocent students returning from holiday bliss.

One of al-Qaeda's motives has been a high kill ratio. In the case of the WTC, 19 trained terrorists killed 3000 innocent people, or a kill ratio of 1 to 150. The recent FBI warnings predicts that the al-Qaeda terrorists network is likely planning something even bigger, inferring a higher kill ratio and more terror than 1 to 150.

If 10 terrorist teams of 2 terrorists each are able to wire up 10 large high school buildings that normally house at least 2,000 students each (thus excluding smaller bungalow or annex type sites), then they could potentially achieve a kill ratio of 20 to 20,000, or 1:1000, and thus cause great panic and socio-economic chaos.

Certainly, law enforcement has been strained and stretched to its limits, as resources have not caught up with need. In addition to keeping an eye on monuments, skyscrapers, bridges, electrical grid, water supplies, rail, nuclear facilities, and ports, etc., I hope we will keep a closer eye on large schools where thousands of our beloved children congregate on a daily basis. Otherwise,

Columbine may end up looking like a drop in the bucket by comparison.

I hope the experts at the highest levels of our national government are advising our great President George W. Bush on the development of a "BUSH DOCTRINE" to protect our great and wonderful nation and the entire western hemisphere against terrorism, narco-terrorism, and renegade groups, organizations, and terrorists states.

God bless America, and may we remain united against the forces of evil, in honor of the memory of untold numbers of great Americans who died to protect our liberty, freedoms, and way of life, and in honor of the great sacrifices of our public safety and military communities.

Sincerely,

A Loyal 911 American
loyal911american@netscape.net

To the Department of Homeland Security, and the FBI

Dear Governor Ridge, and the FBI Director

Our government must become experts in understanding the 3Ts if America is going to win this "War on Terrorism." The **3Ts** are *terrorist targeting tactics.*

1. **Terrorist**. They are the extremists who are willing to commit suicide because they value death more than life, and they hate America more than they love living. They want to be martyrs; to gain the self-respect in death that they don't feel will ever be possible in life. They think they have a cause worth dying for, which will make their families, friends, and commanders proud. Of course, they'll cite from the Koran or whatever to justify their inhumane ways.

2. **Targeting**. Few international terrorists, even those who are already here in America as students, visitors, workers, or illegally really know the back roads in our great country. It's like the terrorists who went to the gym, but exercised in their street clothes. They don't really have a clue what it's like to be American; therefore they look all too obvious and don't "fit in". All that foreign terrorists know about America are the well-publicized symbols that they've seen on television and in the movies, thinking that these icons must represent American wealth and power, and in a significant manner defines our society.

They also know that taking down popularly known symbols like the WTC have a greater emotional impact than taking out unknown rural area targets. In addition to symbolic and popular value, targets would ideally support their zealous anti-Semitic, pro-Islamic, and anti-American beliefs. It is terribly clear, that terrorists want the biggest "bang" for the buck, and they prefer killing as many people as possible, consequently, large cities are their primary targets, as it also gives them a chance to blend in and escape, which they can't easily do in the rural heartland and back roads of "redneck" militia counties.

Of course, high value assets, symbolic of our democracy and world power, such as large public buildings (especially federal), major utilities such as nuclear power plants, major railroad stations and large bus terminals, major airports, dams, the very long and vulnerable California aqueduct and fresh water lakes that supply large cities like Los Angeles, are tempting first strike targets. Also, Las Vegas, internationally known as a shining gem, and symbolic of America's excesses (which they secretly envy) is vulnerable. Of course, they would love to strike at our military bases, as they've done in the past, if for no other reason than as a payback for our bombing the crap out of their camels in Afghanistan.

Consequently, a priority-targeting list would first include major buildings, bridges, stadiums, and shopping malls that tend to have large attendances, especially where larger populations of Elite people might work, shop, or play. Where are the largest Elite populations in America? As far as foreigners know, its New York or Beverly Hills.

3. **Tactics**. The news media and government officials keep reminding Americans that the terrorists' primary goal is to make us afraid of them. Actually, creating fear is a collateral outcome, and not the goal. Their goal is to kill as many of "their enemy" as possible, with the least number of casualties to them. Right now, the scoreboard is 19 terrorists, and 3000 American citizens and residents. If they can maintain this "kill ratio", at the cost of $200,000 per operation, then basic math will suggest a ten-fold increase to $2,000,000 will buy them nuclear or weaponized

bio/chem capacities. A ten-fold increase will cost them 190 of their "soldiers", and kill 30,000 more Americans. You know where this logic is going, before Americans will want our military to nuke Iran.

They also have ulterior motives, as they're playing "chess", making moves to set us up to do predictable actions, which they then take advantage of in attempting to unite the Islamic world, with their terrorist organizations taking a major role in a new Islamic coalition that they plan will be against the West. Successfully striking down American icons and killing thousands of people demonstrates one thing only THAT THEY CAN, with relative impunity. In the face of continuous bombing by the greatest power in the history of the world, they want to prove that they are willing to SUFFER, and to PAY ANY COST TO EVENTUALLY WIN.

They are using the West, particularly America, as a tool to unite the Islamic world in hopes of causing the Jihad, the final Holy War, described in their Quran, and in western Bibles as the Battle of Armageddon. As long as they keep our mindset and actions in the "reactive" mode, then they stand a much better chance of proving their agenda to their Islamic brotherhood, who are actually their choice PRIME AUDIENCE. What can the West do once Saudi Arabia and other oil producing Arab states decide to turn off the oil supply to the developed world?

That is their real motive, to infect the thinking of Arab people, to cause great instability among the dirt poor Arabs in wealthy Arab nations ruled by small autocratic and privileged groups, in the hope of fomenting revolutions. Their real targets are to cause the downfall of governments in Saudi Arabia, Egypt, and Pakistan, thinking that once the existing regimes who are friendly to the West are ousted, the remaining radical anti-American regimes will unite, and destroy Israel, while the West will be impotent to stop them, short of an all-out thermal nuclear war. Perhaps we should order more than the 3,000 advanced jet fighters scheduled to be on line by 2008. Maybe we'll need 3,000 more.

So how can our government stop this insidious disease of international extremist Muslim-led terrorism? Afghanistan is the testing ground to prove both the resolve and courage of the West and America, or to show our weaknesses to the Islamic world. If we make our performance and effectiveness in Afghanistan the focus of our anti-terrorist efforts, then getting bin Laden "dead or alive" locks us into a dilemma that threatens to overturn our shield of irresistible power. If we fail to get the goods (the bad ones in this case), then the poor Islamic zealots all over the world, in over 50 nations, will gain hope and strength. They might even think they could overthrow their governments who are friendly to the West. They may even be able to seize Pakistan's nuclear weapons, as few as they are.

How many Americans are we willing to sacrifice to get bin Laden and his Taliban protectors? Do Americans have the stomach after Vietnam and Iraq to fight to the finish? With the answer to this question is the winner of the war.

Chapter Four – The Weapons

1. **Anthrax.** It is likely a single nut who has (had) access to a microbiology lab at a renowned university, or from a government lab has been culturing anthrax. He (most likely a white male with a bone to pick with the government, like McVey) can culture anthrax in a home lab (like his bathroom) simply by using petri dishes that he takes from work, or buys at lab supply houses. To make lots of anthrax takes time, lots of petri dishes, right temperature and ambient light settings, all not impossible even in a rudimentary lab set up. Then, he can buy fine talcum power and mix the anthrax. Using the proper gas mask, plastic trash bag designed as a biohazard suit (using plastic packing tape to plug gaps), and wearing triple latex gloves that are taped closed to his bio-suit, he can extract spores from the petri dishes, then drop into a container filled with talcum powder. He can then place the anthrax mix into preaddressed envelopes, and wet to seal the envelopes.

He then can place the envelopes into self-sealing plastic bags (doubled-lined). Then he washes his sink with anti-bacterial soap, and washes himself down in the shower, after which he disrobes from the biohazard suit, and places it all into double lined trash bags for disposal. He then disinfects his shower, and takes a shower in the buff to make sure all spores have been washed away.

One night, he sneaks the plastic bags to a local mailbox, wearing latex gloves underneath leather gloves, and then holding his breath, he takes out the envelopes, and drops them into the mailbox. He drops the plastic bags in a trash can, and removes his gloves and disposes them in the nearest public trash receptacle. He returns home, takes another shower with anti-bacterial soap. Right now, he's probably growing more anthrax for the next time he's pissed off, and until our government catches him, he'll continue to be a danger. But what's more scary is, all the terrorists in the world know this is an easy and cheap way to make a bio-weapon that's effective, redundancy security procedures must be in place at these registered labs (must be government listed), using technology to limit access through retinal scans, infrared sensors, and camera surveillance. Alarms must go off when sensors pick up dangerous microbes outside of the secured and bio-quarantine lab areas, causing the entire facility to lock down.

2. **Briefcase sized nukes.** It's not likely terrorist can get large mega tonnage nukes because the only nations with large yield nukes are Russia, China, India, Pakistan, and NATO. North Korea and Israel surely have small yield tactical nukes, and we suspect Iran is working hard to get some nukes. Perhaps a few other nation-states may have nukes too they purchased from the Soviets during their economic meltdown, but those are probably of a tactical yield of under 50 kiloton (Hiroshima yield). A brief case or backpack-sized nuke would have around a 30-40 kt yield, and destroy an area of about 15 miles squared (225 sq.mi.).

Delivery of a small tactical yield nuke through non-military means can be as simple as the following:

a. Send along with baggage on passenger jetliner, as freight on commercial delivery service (UPS, Fedex, etc.), as part of freight in cargo containers aboard ships, as baggage on a cruise ship that is boarding at a busy port of call, on board a civilian small plane, or in any car or truck that crosses our borders.

b. Using a redundancy system, the trigger is connected to an actuator that is powered by one cell phone that is turned on by another cell phone. Consequently, the first cell phone call powers a signal to the first cell phone, which turns on the second cell phone. Then the second call to the second cell number actuates the Polonium 210 nuclear trigger (Soviet old school portable nuke technology) to detonate the tactical nuke. In this way, a "wrong" number call to the second cell number prematurely can be averted because the trigger cell is not powered until the nuke is over the intended target. The call can then be made anytime the portable nuke is in position.

c. A nuke will vaporize all evidence of origin, so there won't be any microscopic sized chips to determine anything (unlike Lockerby). The only evidence might be a "nuclear signature", and blast pattern that would give us an idea of the type and yield of nuke, and who could have had access to that type of weapon. The only known groups to have had access to briefcase nukes is the US and USSR (both programs discontinued), however it is alleged that the Israelis and Chechens may have obtained nuclear weapons from corrupt Soviet generals during the break up of the Soviet Union. and leaves the anonymous culprit at large for future strikes. Terrorists know that they don't need to kill themselves to commit their dastardly acts, as they can do it anonymously.

Suitcase Nukes and Tactical Nuclear Weapons

Al-Qaeda's quest for nuclear weapons commenced in 1996 and he is reported to have spent millions of dollars on this project; The focus has been an acquisition of nuclear suitcase bombs. Arab intelligence sources indicate acquisition of tactical nuclear weapons also. Corroborative evidence has reached United States from Russia, Arab countries, and from confessions by captured Islamic terrorists worldwide. The estimates of Osama bin Laden acquisitions are as follows:

> **Russian estimates**; Few nuclear suitcase bombs.
> **Arab intelligence sources**; More than 20 nuclear suitcase bombs. The nuclear suitcase bombs have been acquired from **Central Asian Republics** (CAR) Islamic countries with the active assistance of Chechen Muslim rebels. Al-Qaeda's agents are reported to have paid $30 million cash and two tons of Afghan heroin worth $700 million in Western markets, to Chechen mafia for this purpose. The suitcase nuclear bombs are reported to be stored at two locations in Afghanistan: In deep tunnels. Kandahar, in deep caves This nuclear program is being run by a Western educated Arab nuclear scientist, (turned Islamic Jehadi) and assisted by five Turkoman Muslim; Others too have been brought from CAR countries.

The nuclear suitcase bombs could only be operated by SPETZNAZ (Russian Special Forces) personnel. Some Ukrainian and Baltic region SPETZNAZ troopers are reported to have been recruited, not for operating the bombs but as escorts/protection for these bombs and the technicians.

However the operational use of suitcase nuclear bombs will be entrusted only to Islamic Jehadis. To overcome the technical problems of coded transmissions for activation of these nuclear suitcase bombs (Russian technique,) it is reported that Laden's nuclear experts could hot-wire them and these can be used by human-bomb volunteers from amongst the Islamic Jehadis seeking martyrdom. That nuclear suitcase bombs could have reached Osama bin Laden stand corroborated by General Lebed; (former Security chief of Russia) statement in 1997 that a number of such bombs stood missing from Russian arsenals.

Combating terrorism is itself a very complex and frustrating task. The task of combating Islamic Jehadi terrorism of the Osama bin Laden variety imposes new challenges for countries being targeted by Islamic Jehadis. The WMD threat so posed can only be effectively met by intelligence of a very high order; which could facilitate pre-emptive actions.

If the current record of Taliban's attitudes to intentional criticism over the Bamiyan episode is an indicator, Osama bin Laden will have nothing but contempt for any overtures to give up the WMDs as a tool of Islamic Jehad. WMDs give the Islamic Jehadis an unprecedented power to indulge in political blackmail of Western and other targeted countries. Aware of the vulnerability of civilised societies to political terror and panic, the WMD provides a heady intoxication of unrivalled power to the Islamic Jehadis.

Do terrorist groups possess nukes?

Institute of Peace and Conflict Studies
Author = Dr.Subhash Kapila, Date: April 12, 2001
http://www.ipcs.org/issues/articles/489-ter-kapila.html

International Terrorism: Osama bin Laden and Weapons of Mass Destruction

The United States and Western Countries have been haunted ever since the disintegration of the Soviet Union with the prospect of WMDs falling into the hands of terrorist groups. Their fears have turned out true with information now available that the Islamic Jehadi groups once led by Osama bin Laden have indeed acquired WMDs. WMDs in the hands of Islamic fundamentalist terrorists fortified with the spirit of martyrdom and imbued with the frenzy of expelling the United States from the Islamic world or Islamisation of countries with sizeable Muslim population, indeed become frightening weapons of terror. Indications of possession of WMDs by Osama bin Laden are amplified below:

Chemical and Biological Weapons

Islamist terrorists, both Afghan and Arab Afghans under the guidance of Osama bin Laden and supervision of Pakistan' ISI have established well fortified facilities in Kandahar in

Afghanistan for production of chemical, bacteriological and radiological weapon (perhaps) too. This set-up was established in May 1998 with the acquisition of plant and machinery from Yugoslavia. This plant arrived via Pakistan with assistance of ISI. The first WMD base at Kandahar commenced training of terrorist operatives for biological and chemical weapons from Pakistan, Bangladesh, Afghanistan. Egypt and the Gulf states there after.

The second WMD base is reported to have been established at Zenica in Bosnia-Herzegovina; Terrorist operative training here is being imparted to first generation European Muslims convertees and second generation emigres from the Muslim world. Sources from which chemical and biological weapons materials/samples have been obtained or purchased for relatively small amounts of money are as follows:

Russia; Viruses causing deadly diseases such as Ebola and Salmonella;

Czech Republic; Samples of botulism bio-toxin;

North Korea; Samples of deadly anthrax;

Unknown Source; Sarin The production facilities are supervised by a group of Ukrainian experts (chemists and biologists).

Technical means for long distance disablement of such weapons do not seem to be in existence. Devoid of these, the United States as the primary target has no choice but to keep strict and effective surveillance of al-Qaeda's activities, the Taliban in Afghanistan and Pakistan as the main conduit of both westward and eastward movement of the Jehadi's WMDs. India too as one of the targets identified by al-Qaeda needs to ponder seriously as to how combat this menace.

Chapter Five – Anti-Terrorism

How can our government protect Americans against this hidden scourge of international and domestic terrorism that demands law enforcement interdiction 100% of the time while terrorists can randomly strike to create terror and economic turmoil even just once as evidenced on 911.

We must adopt and maintain vigilance and take proactive steps to ward off terrorist attacks whenever possible... even though it is impossible to prevent such attacks all the time.

> **Taking Them To Task**, the **4Ts**. The longer all this "war" takes, the stronger they grow in galvanizing Arab support from around the world, and causing instability in Islamic lands whose governments are currently friendly to us. We need more security.

1. Identifying potential terrorist cells
    a) Face print technology must be installed at all points of entry to the U.S.A.
    b) Islamic and Arab foreign students and residents who have resided in America post Desert Storm should be subject to some form of cursory investigation, at the minimum, and in more depth if suspicion arises.
    c) All universities must submit the names and addresses of all foreign

students from the Middle East, who have been studying subjects that expose them to sensitive technologies, such as:

1) chemistry
2) biochemistry
3) nuclear physics
4) structural engineering
5) aviation training
6) truck driving of "big rigs"

4) A cross-check of such students should be matched against other students of a similar background to determine if their contacts are of a suspicious nature. For example, a graduate school chemistry student consistently associating with students of aviation and trucking.

b. Protecting our borders

1) Again, Faceprint technology is essential at all border entries, ports of call, and international airports.
2) A border pass I.D. card with a verifiable thumbprint, or iris recognition system must be employed.
3) There must be 100,000 additionally trained "sniff dogs" to spot the potential transport of explosive materials or drugs at our borders, and

major public buildings.

4) Geiger counters must be installed along all major highways, railways, border crossings, and ports of call to detect for nuclear devices.

c. Protecting our infrastructure

1) Apply new technologies to detect weapons of mass destruction, and install at every major "hub" distribution postal facility.

2) Picowave irradiation of all mail passing through the facility, and portable units to irradiate all equipment, mailbags, tubs, and bin.

3) Hire better trained security, equipped with sensors and dogs to patrol, observe, and protect.

4) Cameras in all potential target areas that are monitored by trained security personnel, who may turn on listening devices in the event of suspicious activities.

There are other things we must do to protect ourselves from this terrorist scourge on humanity. But it will require sacrifice and giving up more of our rights, especially that of privacy. We may one day have to inject a pin-sized computer chip into every resident in America, whether citizen or foreigner, to allow satellites to track and find suspected terrorists. But that might not be necessary, if we can get a handle on what's happening now to bring our lives back to normalcy, to free us from the consuming twangs of fear, and to restore our sense of national security to have freedom of movement, assembly, and commercialism.

Prevention

Prevention is the best solution is to keep this horrible scenario from happening.

a. There should be a 15-mile radius "no fly zone" over our nation's capital, buildings, and on-ground radiation detectors to form a 15 miles radius.
b. An underground "blast proof mall" should be built, with underground fast rail systems from the White House, Congress (both houses), the Pentagon, Supreme Court, and major government departments. This underground government mall must have all communications abilities.
c. Radiation detection over flights on a regular basis of our borders, ports, and airports. Radiation detectors at all border crossing, airports, and ports of call.
d. In the ground radiation detectors in all federal highways, tied to a camera surveillance system that takes video and still photos of any vehicle that triggers the detector, and alerts law enforcement.
e. In flight radiation detection (fly along side) of all commercial jets and ships once they cross within 100 miles off shores.

3. Employees are the most important first security link for our public. They must have the proper training, be vigilant, and genuinely concerned for public safety. That means the food vendors, janitors, security screeners, baggage handlers must all have FBI background checks to weed out the criminals who may steal from baggage, place poison onboard food carts, or place bombs in cargo holds of jets. Everyone must do their part to protect Americans from further atrocities.
4. Our government must invest the required capital and resources in an effective and efficient manner to provide cost-effective and cost-efficient protection of the public, with a minimal level of constitutional violations. Where national security would not be violated, our government must be honest with citizens; otherwise, it will lose credibility when most needed later.
5. The news media must attempt to be objective and broad in its coverage, and not give in to becoming a propaganda tool of the military-industrial complex. Our democracy can only survive when an inquisitive, courageous, and unintimidated national news corps gives the real news to our people. Americans are not weak wimps. We can handle the truth.

Take for instance if the Hubble telescope spots an alien invasion fleet of ETs headed our way, and it would take them a decade to reach Earth, then the American public and the world should know about it, so we can get everyone on board to prepare for the fight. I don't think there will be mass panic, or a break down in Christianity because future events have already been foretold in the Holy Bible. As you know, public reaction all depends on "the media spin".

6. The truth shall set us free. Without truth, there is no real freedom, because we would simply be living in the matrix, an illusion. We must deal with reality, so we can see evil for what it really is, evil. When we remain sheltered in our imaginary bubbles, we may feel happier for the moment. But one day, reality hits us in the face, and we haven't prepared how to deal with uncertainty and atrocities. For example, what were bin Laden's immediate objectives on his attacks on American symbols of financial and military power?

a. He had bought stocks "short", and wanted to make the stock market take a dive, so he could buy low and repay his debts, earning hundreds of millions in profit.

b. It is unlikely that all 50+ siblings could all disown bin Laden and at least a few have been secretly supporting him (who else in his family sold stock high before 911, then bought it back low?).

c. Some feel the body must sacrifice a limb to save the rest of the body. Is that what's going on in our nation right now? Are there plans to allow events to happen, or to cause them that would justify our going after Iraq next?

d. Once we have the Caspian Sea through Afghanistan oil pipeline, and ousted Sadam Hussein, thus placing their oil production "on-line", then would the West feel less worried about the price of oil? And could the major oil companies then work together to insure reasonable costs to consumers? Or will the manipulation of supply and costs be used to entice or punish nation-states to follow the world peace paradigm that will eventually be proposed by the one world government of the future?

e. So what's so bad about a benevolent one-world government, who takes a paternalistic and protective attitude toward the people of the world? Certainly a singular world government can outlaw intolerance, especially racism, ethnic genocide, religious fanaticism, and other "isms". A one-world government can better plan for the proper distribution of global assets, to prevent hunger, to stabilize market prices, to develop the riches of Africa and other underdeveloped parts of the world.

A singular world government, based upon American ideals of equality, freedom, justice, and fairness can be a Godsend blessing to the entire world. Our small planet must evolve from the inter fighting between peoples and nation-states, to be able to effectively address pressing environmental and ecological problems of an international scope, that if not solved, will endanger every human being on Earth, which could lead to human extinction during this century. Effective solutions are not possible as long as there is no single voice in how the evolution and sensible development of our planet should take place. And there can be no single voice, as long as there is no single world government, because all nations will be too selfish to care about other nations and other peoples. We need a daddy to keep the family of mankind together, to act as a peacemaker, mentor, and protector. Let's just do it. The sooner the better.

e. Greed. The only major obstacle that keeps people from accepting, and perhaps embracing the idea of a singular world government is the general perception that the Elites are greedy, as if the poor masses would not be the same, given the opportunity. But the facts also show that some of the most benevolent philanthropists of our time have been industrialists, and wealthy Elites. Poor and uneducated people don't usually have the ability, knowledge, perspective, or intellectual capacity to cause human progress. Sure there've been a few great proletarian leaders, but almost all of them have had western philosophical educations, and were themselves Elites from their own lands. The progress of modern man has come on the backs of the intelligentsia, the wealthy, the socially connected, who used politics as one means to shape society, in responding to economic and social need as expressed by the people. America has come a long way, and is indeed a shining example of freedom, courage, justice, and progress for the entire world to see. Now, we should do a better job to spread our values to the rest of humanity, so they can have a chance to appreciate the great ideals that has made America the greatest nation in the history of mankind.

g. Patriotism and ethical conduct. We need to teach both, beginning from preschool onwards. Much of our nation's problems stem from the lack of both. Let's see how. A patriot would feel appreciative of the great sacrifices previous generations have made to insure our freedoms and rights. A patriot would feel gratitude for the hundreds of thousand of soldiers who died for our nation, to keep us free. A patriot therefore would make sure their actions and lives would honor the memories of all who made untold sacrifices to defend our land against peril and evil.

Consequently, a real patriot would not engage in criminal acts that deprive other Americans of their rights and liberties. A true patriot would not take actions against the government that has protected us all these years, and brought us out of the Great Depression and WW2, but instead would address any differences in opinions through lawful means, and through the ballot box.

Ethical conduct is a fleeting concept. Too many people routinely tell lies on a daily basis, and aren't even aware of it. If people can't be honest in their relationships, then layers and layers of deception develop to distort the truth, which is reality. If people can't be honest in their everyday lives, how can they expect government and our leaders to be honest in their daily dealings? Sure the public holds public office holders to higher ethical and moral standards, as the Clinton impeachment demonstrates, but guess where all our leaders originally came from before they became powerful? And where did all of our wealthy Elites come from before they became wealthy? They came from schools, and learned about ethics and patriotism one way or another. It's time our schools did more to insure our freedoms and way of life, by including patriotism and ethics as important parts of the national core school curriculum.

I wish you both, our President, military, and government Godspeed. I hope you will continue to engender the support of the American people and the international community to rid this world of the scourge of terrorism, so that our future generations and we will be able to live in safety, freedom, and have the chance for a good life. Thank you very much for your dedication.

God bless America, the land of the brave. Let freedom ring, here and all over the world.

Our homeland and military are exposed to many areas of vulnerability, and I have mentioned just the "tip of the iceberg." Mega-greed knows no loyalty to nation, culture, ideals, or people. Greedy people are hypocrites, serpents, and a brood of vipers. To those who worship money, the ends justify the means, and they are fully capable of employing any means necessary to achieve their greedy financial goals. Terrorism, drug dealing, illegal arms trade, mega-corporate mergers, political corruption and investment scams are just the tools that are employed to derive their ill gotten wealth. A house divided can not stand long, consequently the multi-pronged attacks against fundamental American institutions continue to go unabated, and except for the courageous efforts of the CIA and other key agencies, our enemies can weaken us by monitoring or controlling key communication and administration hubs that compromise our military, political, economic, social, and international relations institutions and personnel. Our enemies have a common agenda to bring America down.

How can the CIA rise to the occasion to neutralize our enemies and so-called self-benefiting and disloyal friends, who continue to attack and spy on America? It's a big job, and it won't be easy, but no other agency has the loyalty, guts, resources, talent, and ability to fight the fight. Only the CIA can save America, because you are an honest and patriotic public servant who commands a group of highly trained, patriotic, and loyal people. Globalization and the rapid rise of MNCs, elitist CEO's and oligarchs signal the rapid demise of ethics, morality, patriotism, and humanitarianism. We need not look too far to the event horizon to see our potential futures destroyed by international carpetbaggers and terrorists. We must win a secret war on the secret financiers of global terror soon, otherwise it will be too late for us and our children's generation.

Anti-terrorism requires a positive and proactive mindset. President Bush sent our military into Iraq as an assertive step to combat and prevent future terrorism, whether WMDs were found or not, it was probably just a matter of sooner versus later. The same principle is bearing out in Syria, Iran and North Korea... that eventually they will underestimate America's resolve and make those stupid fatal chess moves that leads to checkmate.

The Bush Doctrine was one of national confidence to put terrorist states and the groups they support on notice. It was a peace imperative that by use of force, Americans were willing and able to enforce the peace. Following is an analogy on how peace and prosperity could be ushered in to the Americas.

The Peace Imperative: The Bush Doctrine

A great leader recognizes that it is the power of persuasion to build consensus among supporters to act as a team, which is the basis of enduring influence and power. Great leaders also recognize that there are moments when they are able to see an uncommon vision, because their heads are above the crowd. At those times of clarity, when followers are hesitant to follow because they can not see the same vision, such as those we elect to occupy and to carry out the greatest leadership role as President of the

United States of America, great leaders are called upon to exercise distinguished courage to stand on principle and rationality. There are situations when great leaders and Presidents may have to stand alone, and to issue unpopular or controversial directives to the nation, its people and military. In most cases, great Presidents are able gain approval by transferring their vision to supporters and to our nation's people.

The world of humans has always been violent, and warfare at times almost appears to be natural selection at work in the grand Darwinian process of survival of the fittest. Civilizations rise and fall, as do leaders, and people become extinct cultures and races at some point in their evolution. Terrorism is the current modality for disgruntled groups to attempt to increase their stake holds in a world system that leaves the vast majority of the human race in the Middle-Ages of poverty, ignorance and powerlessness.

America has been called upon time and time again to solve the world's problems, and now our President leads all Americans in the fight for our survival against global terrorism. President George W. Bush has shown himself to be a capable leader who is up to the sworn duty to protect America first, above all else. Consequently, any actions that he feels are necessary to bring about the end to terrorism would be justifiable, depending upon the scope and enormity of the external and internal threats to domestic order and national economic survival.

President Bush has demonstrated his wisdom and adeptness at building coalitions, synthesizing ideas of his top advisors, and seriously considering the admonitions of his critics. Perhaps time is nearing when President Bush may be called upon to declare a new anti-terrorism doctrine, a hemisphere protection philosophy, or simply, "The Bush Doctrine." The Bush Doctrine, in the honored tradition of the Monroe Doctrine, would spell out the anti-terrorism vision, principles, and mitigating circumstances to the entire world, and draw a deep line in the dirt to terrorist groups, terrorist states, and our potential adversaries, in addition to building solidarity among our existing and potential allies.

The primary tenets of the Bush Doctrine would be:

SECTION 1: VISION

Section 1A) The Western Hemisphere must become a terrorism-free zone in order to permit peaceful social order, economic advancement for all people, inter-cultural exchange, and encourage hemispheric trade.

Section 1B) After the scourge of terrorism has been eradicated, residents of the western hemisphere should have the freedom to move freely between nations in the hemisphere, without fear of harassment, incarceration, or exploitation, as long as conducting lawful activities.

SECTION 2: PRINCIPLES

Section 2A) Random or strategic violence against innocent people and defenseless civilian targets is abhorrent, and must be condemned as "cruel acts against humanity," and must be outlawed by international law, similar to the Geneva Conventions.

Section 2B) Warning and Negotiations: Should any group or state feel compelled to use violence against the civilian populations of other states, they must first announce their intentions and reasons for desiring a military option. The announcement of intentions must first be delivered by videotape to the targeted state's government, and within 24 hours to the international news media. This permits diplomats an opportunity at statesmanship, and to attempt to understand and propose solutions to the grievances.

Section 2C) Self-Defense: Any state or group that engages in military actions against another, without first satisfying Section 2B (above) before the full assemblage of the UN, would be considered an international renegade. Any state that is attacked has the right to respond with military force, and to exert the will of the prevailing hemispheric powers to remove the "renegade group or government by any means necessary," in order to minimize "collateral damage" to the general population, and to restore peace.

SECTION 3: CONSENSUS

The nations within the Western Hemisphere are asked to enjoin in a hemispheric protection agreement, where each nation-state would contribute proportionately in funds, resources, and soldiers to fight hemispheric terrorism, as long as two-thirds of its members agree to specific actions.

SECTION 4: NARCO-TERRORISM

Section 4A) It is recognized that the narcotics trade is not only detrimental to social order and social progress, but has been and is utilized to fund terrorist acts, terrorists recruitment, and terrorists training. Consequently, the members of the Western Hemispheric Alliance agree to coordinate efforts and resources to fight narco-terrorism wherever it may exist in the hemisphere.

Section 4B) Where existing or future narcotics traffickers and criminal organizations are apprehended and proven to facilitate, support, finance, or trade with terrorist groups, terrorist organizations, or terrorist states, the full effect of R.I.C.O. will apply, and the penalties at conviction will be doubled.

Section 4C) Where such criminal groups referred to in Section 4B (above) cooperate with the hemispheric alliance, and identify terrorist groups, targets, and facilities, their punishment will be reduced by at least 50 percent, or more.

SECTION 5: OTHER PROVISIONS

Several other major areas would deal with immigration, trade, military cooperation and other aspects required to fight and eradicate terrorism, and to provide a prolonged peace.

Leadership that defines a clear vision, principles, and strategies that all can understand, though not necessarily agree, would provide justification for constructive engagements. Justification does not require unanimity, but must provide a rational and deliberate humanitarian basis for military actions.

Subsequent to the formation of a united Western Hemispheric Alliance, the "war on terrorism" would be infused with greater effectiveness, resources, depth, and breath to fight terrorism in their own backyards. Peace in the hemisphere and in the world requires decisive command that serves a global vision of social order and economic progress for all peoples.

The Display of Patriotism Immediately After 9/11/01

The American public has a large part to play in the fight against terrorists and terrorism as they are large in numbers and can be the eyes and ears of a vigilant but confident people. America and the world witnessed an upsurge in patriotism all over the US in the months subsequent to the tragic terrorist attacks on the World Trade Center and the Pentagon. Many Americans heard the call for action, and despite some trepidation, the vast majority of Americans supported our courageous leaders, military, and public safety people to begin the fight against global terrorism and terrorist states who encourage, finance, and harbor terrorists.

President Bush asked the American people to join in the fight against terrorist, and to help. In the weeks and months that followed, Americans sent emails and faxes to our President, Senators, news media, the FBI, Department of Homeland Security, and other law enforcement agencies. Americans proposed various ideas, similar to "The Three 'Ts'" that described terrorist tactics, and "The Four 'Ts'" that described tactics our government could use to fight terrorism, which included "Taking the Fight to Them." Our military, government agencies and first responders proposed to support our President by implementing The Bush Doctrine, which takes the fight to the heartland of the terrorists, so we would not have to fight them on our homeland.

The issue of patriotism has taken on a negative context in the years following the Viet Nam War, with the news media, anti-war activists, liberals, and left-wing legalists who attack our Constitution, and an entire generation of college professors have attempted to brainwash our students to reject plain ol' American patriotism. Flag waving, reciting the Pledge of Allegiance, and open displays of patriotism became equated with being a "right-winger", which was a coded word that was equated with being racist. But immediately following 911, Americans from all walks of life, native born and immigrants alike, all felt what it really means to be an American, and to live in a great democracy with legal protections of our individual freedoms. We were proud, and we were not going to let a few terrorists take that away from us. We were not going to cower before the world over a big bloody nose. We were going to fight back, whenever, wherever, and whatever it takes, and however long until the scourge of terrorism is eliminated. We went into Afghanistan, then Iraq.

Our military victories were swift, with minimal lost of life to our troops (just compare to all other wars!), and civilian populations in the war zones. Naturally, we expected the policing and rebuilding portion subsequent to wars almost always takes more time, expense, effort, and sometimes additional lost of lives. And we are witnessing that now.

President Bush is right. We will not run! One of the major reasons Bin Laden felt he could attack America was because the world has the impression that the Viet Nam war took away our guts to fight wars against despots. They saw America as a paper tiger, filled with lazy and self-indulgent people. Now that we're proving to the world that Americans have the courage to go the long haul, too many nations criticize the U.S. for being too aggressive! Bull on that.

What is patriotism? It's the feeling of being an American, not in a jingoistic way, but in one's heart and gut. There's no way to explain the feeling, but you know it when you feel it. It's like trying to explain what it feels "to be in love." You only know it when you feel it. And when you feel it, you know it for sure. And so, patriotism is to love one's nation, its people, ideals, and way of life. Certainly, nothing is ever perfect, but people who criticize America are also the same people who are at a loss to name one nation on the face of the earth, or in the entire history of human beings that can come close to the shining example of humanity that has been America! There's an inherent obligation to criticism, that of suggesting a better alternative, choices, improvements, or solutions.

Critics are often like non-voters who want everybody to hear their opinionated political perspectives, which don't change anything as long as they don't participate in the democratic process that sets

America apart from 95% of the world. So next time the "Stars Spangled Banner" is sung at a stadium, stand up proudly, sing loudly, and salute our flag for which it stands.. . bravery, loyalty, freedom and for all our troops who have given their lives to defend America's honor and way of life. Let's all be proud, and say "God Bless America" again and again and again.

President Bush and Homeland Security were correct to raise our national terrorism level to orange-high. We must have immediate concern for the safety of our cities, as Bin Laden has shown his determination to finish jobs, where he had failed on a previous attempt. We shouldn't presume that his latest statements regarding the destruction of an entire American city is merely a bluff or hot air designed to pump up terrorists. He may wish to assist Saddam Hussein take revenge and also inspire international terrorism by attacking key American leaders, buildings, and other symbols. Where possible, the residences of our top leaders and their immediate families must be adequately protected by effective security measures to prevent car or truck bombs, which are the preferred choice of attack by suicidal terrorists.

With the advent of this new millennium, we entered into a new global paradigm, where interrelationships between bankers and stockbrokers become intermingled with the mutual monetary goals of drug cartels, illegal arms merchants, enemy states, corrupt politicians, criminal syndicates, and international terrorists. Diverting legitimate funds often finances the flow of drugs and weapons, with illegal profits washed clean through money-laundering networks abetted by domestic and international banks.

It has become difficult to track down the financiers of terrorism only because on the surface, they appear to be legitimate individuals, usually above suspicion, but occupying high perches from which great financial benefits are derived. The CIA must have access to the latest spy technologies to permit the identification and apprehension of all groups who are a national threat.

Our homeland and military are exposed to many areas of vulnerability, and our current fight is just the "tip of the iceberg." Mega-greed knows no loyalty to nation, culture, ideals, or people. Greedy people are hypocrites, serpents, and a brood of vipers. To those who worship money, the ends justify the means, and they are fully capable of employing any means necessary to achieve their greedy financial goals. Terrorism, drug dealing, illegal arms trade, mega-corporate mergers, political corruption and investment scams are just the tools that are employed to derive their ill gotten wealth.

Globalization and the rapid rise of MNCs, elitist CEOs and oligarchs signal the rapid demise of ethics, morality, patriotism, and humanitarian responsibilities. We need not look too far to the event horizon to see our potential futures destroyed by international carpetbaggers and terrorists. We must win the secret war on the secret financiers of global terror soon, otherwise it will be too late for our children's generation and us.

Hopefully, it's not too late to prevent Bin Laden from exploding nukes in our cities, as he has boasted he plans to do. No security system invented can indefinitely safeguard 100 percent against attacks from determined terrorists, especially when America is an open target due to our liberties and freedoms. Unfortunately, there are both foreign nationals and citizens who would become party to mass murder, for a twisted cause or for money.

If al-Qaeda is ever successful in exploding a nuke in our homeland, our government, law enforcement and military must be prepared to take extreme measures against all financiers of terrorism, including supportive nation-states. It is no accident that the major terrorist states who formed the Axis of Evil have suddenly agreed to international monitoring and or dismantling of their nuclear weapons programs. Why have Libya, Iran, and North Korea suddenly, within weeks of each other, agreed to suspend or moderate their nuclear energy development programs? Could it be they have advanced knowledge of the plot by al-Qaeda to nuke US cities; and consequently, they want to be able to deny any culpability, because they can claim their nuclear energy programs are under international inspection, or being dismantled? We need to discover what these suddenly cooperative terrorists and despots know about Al-Qaeda's plot to nuke our cities. We need to discover terrorists communications channels, because as certain as bin Laden was able to send tapes to Al Jezzera, he was forced to rely on others to reach out from his hideout; consequently an opportunity presented itself in his discovery and subsequent execution.

We are spending hundreds of billions on reconstructing Iraq, but we must not forget the more urgent task at home; to discover and neutralize the impending nuclear attack on America. We must give the CIA all the resources that it needs to unearth the dastardly plots being planned by Al-Qaeda and other terrorist groups. Then we must pray that the best, brightest, and bravest CIA agents and personnel will be able to intercede and to prevent the impending execution of any nuclear terrorism.

Finally, we must not blame the CIA in the event Al-Qaeda is able to succeed in mounting a catastrophic attack on our homeland because it is not humanly possible to prevent all attacks, no matter how wide an intelligence net may be projected. In the event our homeland is nuked, our military may need to respond with a formidable counter attack. Should hundreds of thousands or millions of our innocent population are murdered by Bin Laden nukes, our populace will scream for a bloody revenge, which may drive our nation into a new era of pre-emptive military action.

It is obvious that Iran and North Korea want to get off our list of terrorist states, but subsequent to a catastrophic nuclear strike by al-Qaeda, we will need to nuke somebody in response, and that might entail nuking all suspected al-Qaeda strongholds in Afghanistan, Pakistan, Iran, Kashmir, Philippines or wherever they exist. Even if we're not lucky enough to kill all of the terror cells, our reactionary use of nukes will make terrorist states and terrorist sympathizers think twice about providing nuclear weapons and expertise to terrorists. Subsequently, our military will be called on to destroy any attempts to obtain nuclear technology of any type by non-nuclear nation-states, and smaller nuclear nations will be forced to dismantle their nuclear weapons programs. Consequently, the only nuclear nations that will remain will be those who developed nuclear capacity before 1970, leaving Russia, China, Britain, France, and NATO as the only nations permitted to retain their nuclear stockpiles, which should be gradually destroyed and verified by the UN.

In the mean time, let's all go on with living our normal lives, hope for the best, but be prepared as much as humanly possible for the worse case scenarios. And should the worse case scenario occur, we need to muster all of our strength and determination to end the terrorist plight on our planet once and for all. It is not true that one man's terrorist is another man's freedom fighter. The only truth is that unconscionable terrorists are terrorists. Consequently, if attacked, America has the unalienable right to retaliate, using any and all means possible. We must, so help us God.

Dear President Bush...

I know you're much too busy taking care of our nation's urgent business to read the hundreds of thousands of emails and letters pouring in from Americans and from our friends around the world.

I hope your administration will make controlling our borders and immigration a top priority, after hunting down and prosecuting the perpetrators of terrorism. Especially nowadays, immigration and border control is a necessary precondition for the survival of our freedom and way of life in America. We need to do something soon to correct the problems presented to the security of Americans and all residents of the United States by unchecked and open borders.

It is possible terrorists have already hidden nuclear and biological weapons within various cities, in the end other democracies. And like "sleeper" cells, one day, they spring forward without warning to do their dastardly deeds. In WW2, which many Americans have forgotten, the enemy

Japan sneaked attacked Pearl Harbor. After hundreds of thousands of American casualties, we nuked them four years later. A week after the second nuke, Japan surrendered. And now, they are our allies. If we could have developed nuclear capabilities sooner, and we nuked Japan years earlier, it may have save the loss of several millions of lives, including civilians from many nations.

My paternal grandfather was murdered by the Japanese (decapitated, and his body thrown into the creek), and the rest of my family on my Dad's side vanished, except for an uncle and two aunts who got caught in the communist revolution. We have no idea what has happened to my paternal grandmother and relatives who didn't get out of China in time, like we did. If the U.S. could have developed nuclear weapons a mere five years earlier, the Japanese would have thought twice about attacking Pearl Harbor and all of Asia. Consequently, my relatives on my Dad's side would probably still be alive today, as well as millions of innocents and combatants alike and all the
American heroes who gave their lives to fight evil.

My grandfather on my mom's side served in the Army during WW2, as a cook. My uncle served in the Corps of Engineers during the war, and my Dad was a clerk typist for the Army Headquarters in Hong Kong after the War. We were rewarded with immigration to America in 1954, when the entire quota for Asia was 150. My family has always been on the side of America, the land of freedom and opportunity. We proudly became American citizens in 1960.

Nowadays, anyone, even those who hate America are allowed to come onto our shores, and many of these people have loyalties to their homelands, and not to the USA. So why the heck do we let them stay here, and be a potential threat to we Americans? Why do we allow people from nations who openly hate us to learn from our best universities and schools, only later to use their American education to ferment cyber sabotage, chemical, biological, and perhaps even nuclear terrorism?

My only concern is, are we too late to stop this terrorism thing? Do they already have in their possession weapons of mass destruction? Are they ticking time bombs, waiting for the opportunities to strike out against us again? I hope not, but do we know for sure what we might be up against? I worry because, since our government has been somewhat ineffective at stopping the flow of drugs that has been killing our kids, can we be sure they'd do better in stopping smuggling of weapons of mass destruction? The first step to combat these worse case scenarios is to protect our borders from unwanted immigration that has a negative impact on our way of life, security, economy, and infrastructure.

A Canadian newspaper published an editorial after the WTC/Pentagon bombings, as follows:

America: The Good Neighbor.

Widespread but only partial news coverage was given recently to a remarkable editorial broadcast
from Toronto by Gordon Sinclair, a Canadian television commentator. What follows is the full

text of his trenchant remarks as printed in the Congressional Record:

This Canadian thinks it is time to speak up for the Americans as the most generous and possibly the least appreciated people on all the earth. Germany, Japan and, to a lesser extent, Britain and Italy were lifted out of the debris of war by the Americans who poured in billions of dollars and forgave other billions in debts. None of these countries is today paying even the interest on its remaining debts to the United States. When France was in danger of collapsing in 1956, it was the Americans who propped it up, and their reward was to be insulted and swindled on the streets of Paris. I was there. I saw it.

When earthquakes hit distant cities, it is the United States that hurries in to help. This spring,

> *59 American communities were flattened by tornadoes. Nobody helped. The Marshall Plan and the Truman Policy pumped billions of dollars into discouraged countries. Now newspapers in those countries are writing about the decadent, warmongering Americans.*

I'd like to see just one of those countries that is gloating over the erosion of the United States dollar build its own airplane. Does any other country in the world have a plane to equal the Boeing Jumbo Jet, the Lockheed Tri-Star, or the Douglas DC10? If so, why don't they fly them? Why do all the International lines except Russia fly American Planes?

Why does no other land on earth even consider putting a man or woman on the moon? You talk about Japanese technocracy, and you get radios. You talk about German technocracy, and you get automobiles. You talk about American technocracy, and you find men on the moon! - not once, but several times - and safely home again.

> *You talk about scandals, and the Americans put theirs right in the store window for everybody to look at. Even their draft-dodgers are not pursued and hounded. They are here on our streets, and most of them, unless they are breaking Canadian laws, are getting American dollars from ma and pa at home to spend here. When the railways of France, Germany and India were breaking down through age, it was the Americans who rebuilt them. When the Pennsylvania Railroad and the New York Central went broke, nobody loaned them an old caboose. Both are still broke.*

I can name you 5000 times when the Americans raced to the help of other people in trouble. Can you name me even one time when someone else raced to Americans in trouble? I don't think there was outside help even during the San Francisco earthquake.

Our neighbors have faced it alone, and I'm one Canadian who is damned tired of hearing them get kicked around. They will come out of this thing with their flag high. And when they do, they are entitled to thumb their nose at the lands that are gloating over their present troubles. Stand proud, America!

Terrorist Training Theatres

Many Americans had a gut reaction to 911 wanting our government to do more to protect our homeland. Of course, I do not personally wish the wanton killing of innocent people, no matter what country. We should go after the guilty parties, and not the innocent. But, if we're gonna win this "war against terrorism", we should give 100% support to our military, up to and including nuclear capabilities, if necessary. It'll soon be time for decisive and courageous action. We already know the international seats of terrorism:

1. Iran
2. Iraq
3. Libya
4. Syria
5. Palestine
6. Afghanistan

But just what is America and the world going to do about ending the brain trusts and financiers of worldwide terrorism?

First, let's stop worrying about everybody else's problems, and start to concentrate on our own, as the Canadian editorial clearly testifies that no other nation on earth has really come to our aid since the official independence of our republic.

As OUR President, Americans stand united with you to smoke out the terrorists and get them on the run. Then, we need to build the national missile defense. If nothing else, we'll be able to shoot down meteors or nukes from Russian or China (just in case they become hostile in the future). Maybe shoot down UFOs that are on their way to invade earth. Who knows? Then we need to control or close borders. We need to train 100,000 drug and bomb sniffing dogs real soon and put them at all points of entry to the US and at all major buildings and sensitive sites, such as nuclear reactors, pipelines, etc. We also need to install Geiger counters on all major highways to detect the transport of any radioactive materials. Then we need to have our military jets fly along side commercial jet routes and shipping lanes to protect our citizens and property.

Might makes right. Or have we forgotten the lessons of history, the Civil War, WW1, WW2, and Desert Storm? As long as we spend all our time debating, terrorist states and terrorists plan their next assaults on our nation and people. Their goal is to destroy us. And they will if we let it happen. The best defense is a strong and sustained offense, a military 101 basic! Let's kick their ass, and stop licking their butts. If we have to occupy terrorist nations and take their oil as retribution, let's just do it (like Nike says).

Respect comes from fear, and not from kindness. Let's be merciful after we punish them, and bring them to their knees. We must do this for our future generations and make Americans proud again, and not be a bunch of liberal ACLU wimps who feel guilty for saying politically incorrect statements and worry about what everybody else will think. Who the hell cares? Why should we care what Europe, or Asia, or Latin America thinks about us? What have they ever done for us? (Okay, the French did help America during the American Revolutionary War, but what happened in the War of 1812? Anyway, most French hate us nowadays anyway).

The world owes the United States of America. We don't owe the world a damn thing. Sometimes leadership means having the courage to stand up tall, and stand alone to get something done right. If we listen to all the doubters and liberal moralists all the damn time, we wouldn't be able to take a damn crap without worrying we'd be polluting the environment.

It's time to kick butt. I hope the American public will support our military to do their job, and not get us into another Vietnam. History should have taught us some important lessons. If Truman gave McArthur permission to go into China, it would have never turned communist. If elder Bush had permitted Desert Storm to take out Saddam, there would have been no attack against the Pentagon and the World Trade Center (it wasn't just Sammy Ben Ladin). If Jimmy Carter had bombed the hell out of Iran, the Ayatollah would have returned our hostages (instead, Carter and America was humiliated before the international community, which encouraged even worse cases of terrorism). President Clinton had the right idea by sending cruise missiles to Kabul, only he screwed up and forgot to put on nuclear tip warheads.

Let's look to the Bible for some inspiration. Didn't God kill the bad people? They weren't innocent, they were evil, like the terrorists and terrorist states who sponsor them, who also execute Christians, and who bind their own women into a form of slavery, even permitting the execution of women for "dishonoring" the name of the man, whether husband, brother, or father. Where's all the supposed belief in peace from followers of a religion that allows persecution of Christians and outright murder of its own people, not to mention those who they see as evil, like the A. This religious freedom thing can be taken a bit too far by fanatics!

But who leads the world in pursuit of good, and human rights? Is it Iran, Iraq, Syria, Afghanistan, Libya, or other totalitarian Islamic states? NO! It's the good 'ol U.S. of A, again and again, standing up for human rights and the little guy.

I'm damn proud to be an American, and that my family earned the privilege to become loyal Americans. Maybe it's high time to make loyalty to the American form of government, ideals, principles, and way of life a prerequisite for immigration to our great country. After all, isn't the reason most immigrants want to come to America to escape persecution from their homelands, and to gain economic opportunities not allowed over there? It's elementary History 101. Let's get real picky about who we let into our great nation, so they won't spoil it.

Best wishes, and may God bless you and America in these most difficult times. Let freedom ring!

Patriotic Americans come from all races and former nationalities.

When the Spy Plane crash landed in China, many Americans were upset and wanted to send in the Marines. There was even talk of putting Chinese in America, and loyal Chinese-Americans into concentration camps. I'm glad that didn't happen, as things were properly resolved through diplomatic channels.

But this terrorism thing cannot be resolved through diplomatic channels. Terrorists are not legitimate (or even illegitimate) government entities. They are pockets of only hundreds to a few thousand zealots who believe the US is their archenemy. Trying to hunt down and kill cockroaches is not an easy task. You kill a bunch of them, and the eggs survive even the most potent pesticides, hatching later to reinfest. Why do we allow known terrorists to stay in the US while attending American schools to learn skills that they plan to use against us later? Keep them out!

The "free world" has been traumatized by the events on the morning of September 11 in NYC
and DC. While some extremists groups may celebrate the horrific inhumane attacks on innocent
people, Americans have shown the world restraint, and have not singled out any particular ethnic or
racial group for domestic hate crimes.

I was watching the news on Tuesday at 5:30 am/pdt. The news was interrupted at 5:55 am, by a breaking story. The screen flashes to a skyscraper on fire. First I thought it was another action movie... but the commentator stated that witnesses reported a jet flew into the World Trade Center. They were speculating as to the type of plane, and how such an incident could happen on a clear day.

I was perplexed. It was surreal. As I was glued to the TV when suddenly another jet appeared from the right side, then there was another explosion. First I didn't realize there was a second building, as the first one obscured the second. After about ten seconds of puzzlement, a newscaster stated that it appeared a second jet had crashed into the building. They reviewed the video to confirm their observation.

It took another five minutes before the news people figured out it was a second jet slamming into the second tower. I was shocked. I was sickened. I couldn't believe my what my eyes had witnessed.

Of course, I've talked to various people, and while most reactions were sympathy, mixed with anger (one ex-marine buddy of mine said we should nuke 'em, and when I asked nuke who? he blurted out, nuke them damn "sand n**ger camel jockeys". When I asked how we could be sure we were striking out at the guilty parties, he just said, "Who gives a sh*t, we have plenty of evidence, and anyway, we gotta show how strong we are so them damn "rag heads" will know not to f*ck with us again."

Most are more reasonable. Let's do real investigation to make sure we're retaliating against those who are guilty. And a few stated that the US and the First World needs to mitigate the causes that drive people to give up their lives willingly for a "just cause", in terms of their twisted perceptions and beliefs.

One thing has always been obvious to me... much of the Muslim world hates the U.S., and we immigrants are all Americans who reside here, whether we agree with our government's policies or not. From the outside looking in, no matter what we individually think, or our race or ethnicity, history of struggle, etc., other people in other nations see us all as "Americans", and unfortunately, many groups and some nations overtly encourage their populations to hate us. We're not human to them, just the enemy. And that's probably how most Americans feel about "them."

I hope our government will be able to prevent the next levels of terrorism, and do a much better job than they have in the fight against drug cartels. The WTC/Pentagon "bombings" may only be the beginning of terrorists' plans to "up the ante." How can our government and military stop future terrorists from:

1. cyber sabotage of infrastructure
2. biological & viral infestation
3. nuclear detonations
4. genetic genocide

All can be done without the presence of suicidal human conspirators... as "plain" packages aboard ships, trains, planes, busses, cars, or inside buildings, schools, hospitals, and sports stadiums can be detonated by a simple cell phone call.

Force as a response may feel good, but will it then escalate terrorism to a worse level? What are the root causes that must be resolved to prevent more of these types of atrocities? Can we really find the guilty parties and bring them to justice without making them martyrs to their twisted causes? Are these violent episodes indicative of human nature, a history filled with violence, war, and genocide?

Unfortunately, hundreds of unbalanced people have been exploiting the situation, by doing some
wrong things, like calling in bomb scares, making false solicitations of sympathetic Americans for monetary donations for relief efforts

(which never makes it to that purpose), and other unconscionable or devious behaviors. Fortunately, these misguided people are a small number compared to the good that millions of Americans and people around the world are doing on a daily basis. Unfortunately, it was 19 terrorists that took the lives of over 3,000 innocent Americans, and caused over twenty billion dollars of damage to American icons and property, not to mention the disruption and loss of hundreds of millions of dollars in commerce. And it's not possible to measure the profound emotional suffering and personal loss that relatives of the dead, injured and missing must be feeling right now, and will feel well into the future.

Americans and the world grieve for humanity. I pray for all the souls given up in the struggle of good against evil, and for their families and loved ones. I hope America and the free world will win. May God bless America, the free world, and the side of good against evil in this world. This is a reminder of how fragile and uncertain life really is. It is a reminder to show a little more love and concern to our families, friends, neighbors, and communities because we can never know how what could happen in a moment.

Chapter Six – Conclusions

The root causes of terrorism are based upon historical inequities, exploitation, and disrespect for the poor masses that created opportunities for hate-mongers to galvanize and harness that raw energy, resentment and hatred that is the undercurrent of impoverished peoples who see no hope for better lives in the global system of economic inequities. When people have little to nothing, and therefore nothing to lose, the potential sacrifice of their lives to gain the respect and admiration of their countryman becomes more attractive. Terrorist groups, whether espousing religious, ethnic, racial, or political agendas and dogmas are able to effectively focus the hatred of the masses on their common enemies, while utilizing peer-pressure, group identification, intimidation and jingoism to further their agendas against alleged oppressors.

American military forages into Iraq and Afghanistan through regime change in the superficial attempt to install a political system that is foreign to those peoples and lands have been mostly a failure after the cost of several trillion U.S. Dollars, the lost of over 5,000 brave and patriotic American lives, and the physical and emotional trauma and suffering of hundreds of thousands of the "walking dead" and their families as a result of warfare that disrupted their normal lives. In addition, the real damage has been the creation of instability in the Middle-East and the heightening of anti-American and anti-western sentiments among the populace. It is impossible to change "the hearts and minds" of people we are supposedly attempting to liberate, while our bombs are killing their families. It's just that simple. And with every surviving casualty, another new and determined hateful enemy is created.

The fundamental weakness and fault of status quo corporate think tanks is they are made blind by the elitist desire for profits, at any cost of foreign lives and property. Dick Cheney fabricated CIA evidence to trick GWB to go to war with Iraq over WMD's and nukes that simply didn't exist. His company, Halliburton reaped a windfall of multi-billion dollar no-bid logistics and support contracts. WMD's and nukes are the types of weapons in the Israeli arsenal and are held as bargaining chips against the U.S. and its allies. It's because Israeli purchased at fire sale prices old Soviet nukes (bombs, artillery shells, suitcase/briefcase nukes, and polonium 210 nuclear bomb triggers used to bring down the WTC twin towers on 911, so claim various so-called conspiracy theorists) that Islamic jihadists are pursuing nuclear WMD's for their arsenals. Another flaw in elitist thinking is they believe overwhelming might and technological advantage will, at the end of the day, insure victory. Consequently, the spoils will belong to the victor, in addition to reconstruction contracts. It was President Dwight Eisenhower, arguable the greatest American General of all times (and the only 5-star General ever), who as Supreme Commander of Allied Forces during WWII, who defeated both the Nazi and Japanese war machines. He also warned the world against the insidious threat of perpetual wars that benefit those with stake holds in manufacturing false flag wars.

The blind adherence to the belief that profits above honor certainly benefits the believers who personally benefit from war profits without risking their own lives or those of their families. Unfortunately, history has clearly shown that in the long run, after what may seem like generational struggles, eventually, galvanizing leadership and unintended consequences materialize, and then the roosters come home to roost. Every pompous mighty civilization has fallen, with the last being the British. America has exerted global hegemony through economic and military dominance since the collapse of the Soviet Union's economy that contributed to ending the Cold War, however, both Russia and China are increasingly challenging America's claim to the crown.

Arab Spring and regime change in Arab lands demonstrate how relatively easy it is to destabilize and overthrow even the most feared tyrannical governments in the Middle-East. Cut off the head, and the body dies. Unfortunately, the blood letting in Islamic lands disguises an attempt of western oil barons to control oil production and exports from those lands, which if ISIL/ISIS proves effective, will show other jihadists an effective route to retake their homelands. We should expect the expansion of Islamic states, where there were once secular autocratic tyrants. As these oil rich states cash in on their resources through oil contracts with China, whose population and economic pressures drive them to develop global energy resources without regards to local politics or religious beliefs, the U.S. and western allies who cling to ideological and geo-political rationale will likely experience a marked retrenchment in their trade positions and commensurate profits.

Until American politicians, Israelis, and western nations being to recognize the root causes of Islamic hatred toward them, these predominantly Aryan-Caucasian nations stand to suffer retribution in various forms and at unpredictable times. And while Sharia Law certainly curtails personal freedoms in Islamic lands, the result of Islamic terrorism will serve to further restrain the freedoms that western populations have enjoyed and taken for granted.

Is it too late to "win the hearts and minds" in the lands of Mohammed? Is it necessary to even try? While there are no sure fire solutions to these centuries old antagonisms, negotiations at the end of the barrel of the gun is less likely to bring binding peace than agreement that fosters mutual respect and independent development. The natural order of humans and animals clearly segregate along ethnic and species lines. With humans, there are complicating factors such as beliefs that animals don't have to deal with because their natural survival instincts have proven effective for millenniums before the advent of destructive human beings.

Perhaps one way to solve these long lasting ethnic and religious conflicts is to negotiate for a more equitable distribution of wealth, where all natural ethnic groups would be entitled to their own sovereign states. Of course, this solution would only work were governments and their mighty militaries are willing to respect treaties and not to further encroach and land grab other ethnic lands from their native peoples. Unfortunately, the British Empire made a mess of the world, by drawing national boundaries that created nation-states without regards to the existence of traditional ethnic lands. The ethnic conflict that have been experienced in many lands, such as Yugoslavia, Iraq, Ukraine, Kashmir, Tibet, and elsewhere have been a direct consequence of inter-ethnic conflict. For whatever genetic or cultural dispositions, "birds of a feather" prefer to "flock together", and the denial of that basic natural instinct will invariable result in conflict leading to violence and warfare.

Without a rational and binding approach to ethnic and religious violence around the world, the default solution is to let the warring parties fight it out, and the winners take all. Perhaps that's also a natural consequence of life that the Apex Predators will always be on top of the resource hierarchy on Planet Earth. And if that is so, then terrorism is part and parcel to periodic challenges that the "top dogs" will receive from those seeking to exert their own significance and territorial claims to geo-political and economic power in their own perceived spheres of historical influence.

The U.S.A. Patriot Act was passed in response to 911, as a plan to keep Americans safe in our homeland. Since 911, there has been no major organized terrorist attack on American shores, and Homeland Security programs and law enforcement agents have thwarted many sporadic and individually inspired attacks. Now that terrorist groups such as ISIL/ISIS appear to be accessing potentially huge monetary resources and modern U.S. weaponry seized from fleeing Iraqi military forces, the future reach and effectiveness of Islamic jihadists and terrorists are likely to be felt more often, not only in Europe, but right here on the home front in America.

When those inevitable terrorist attacks reoccur, the measured response from our national leaders will determine whether the scourge of terrorism becomes heightened, or if rational minds will prevail, and long-lasting solutions may be found. It may sound like political strength to say "We don't negotiate with terrorists", and "We will pursue them and bring them to justice" and that's a great ideal. But we may someday find that a new reality may force the hands of western nations, to either negotiate to prevent worse scenarios, or to use overpowering military weaponry to create future generations of hate mongers whose lives would be dedicated to the destruction of the west. And while that worse case scenario is highly unlikely, any success of global terrorists keeps hope alive for the downtrodden who see no other avenue than to fight for their chosen way of life. We may see a situation where Second Amendment supporters will prevail, because external attacks by foreign forces only iterate the importance of arming the American public, because when SHTF (shit hits the fan), then it will be time for "Johnny to get his guns" to protect their families and their homeland from foreign invaders... just as foreign fighters have viewed their roles in fighting western invaders and occupiers for the past hundred years.

Appendix:

USA PATRIOT Act as Passed by Congress (abridged version)

Uniting and Strengthening America by Providing Appropriate Tools Required to Intercept and Obstruct Terrorism Act (Oct. 25, 2001)

HR 3162 RDS

107th CONGRESS

1st Session

H. R. 3162

IN THE SENATE OF THE UNITED STATES

October 24, 2001

Received

AN ACT

To deter and punish terrorist acts in the United States and around the world, to enhance law enforcement investigatory tools, and for other purposes.

Be it enacted by the Senate and House of Representatives of the United States of America in Congress assembled,

SECTION 1. SHORT TITLE AND TABLE OF CONTENTS.

(a) SHORT TITLE- This Act may be cited as the `Uniting and Strengthening America by Providing Appropriate Tools Required to Intercept and Obstruct Terrorism (USA PATRIOT ACT) Act of 2001'.

(b) TABLE OF CONTENTS- The table of contents for this Act is as follows:

Sec. 211. Clarification of scope.

Sec. 212. Emergency disclosure of electronic communications to protect life and limb.

Sec. 213. Authority for delaying notice of the execution of a warrant.

Sec. 214. Pen register and trap and trace authority under FISA.

Sec. 215. Access to records and other items under the Foreign Intelligence Surveillance Act.

Sec. 216. Modification of authorities relating to use of pen registers and trap and trace devices.

Sec. 217. Interception of computer trespasser communications.

Sec. 218. Foreign intelligence information.

Sec. 219. Single-jurisdiction search warrants for terrorism.

Sec. 220. Nationwide service of search warrants for electronic evidence.

Sec. 221. Trade sanctions.

Sec. 222. Assistance to law enforcement agencies.

Sec. 223. Civil liability for certain unauthorized disclosures.

Sec. 224. Sunset.

Sec. 225. Immunity for compliance with FISA wiretap.

TITLE III--INTERNATIONAL MONEY LAUNDERING ABATEMENT AND ANTI-TERRORIST FINANCING ACT OF 2001

Sec. 301. Short title.

Sec. 302. Findings and purposes.

Sec. 303. 4-year congressional review; expedited consideration.

Subtitle A--International Counter Money Laundering and Related Measures

Sec. 311. Special measures for jurisdictions, financial institutions, or international transactions of primary money laundering concern.

Sec. 353. Penalties for violations of geographic targeting orders and certain record keeping requirements, and lengthening effective period of geographic targeting orders.

Sec. 354. Anti-money laundering strategy.

Sec. 355. Authorization to include suspicions of illegal activity in written employment references.

Sec. 356. Reporting of suspicious activities by securities brokers and dealers; investment company study.

Sec. 357. Special report on administration of bank secrecy provisions.

Sec. 358. Bank secrecy provisions and activities of United States intelligence agencies to fight international terrorism.

Sec. 359. Reporting of suspicious activities by underground banking systems.

Sec. 360. Use of authority of United States Executive Directors.

Sec. 361. Financial crimes enforcement network.

Sec. 362. Establishment of highly secure network.

Sec. 363. Increase in civil and criminal penalties for money laundering.

Sec. 364. Uniform protection authority for Federal Reserve facilities.

Sec. 365. Reports relating to coins and currency received in non-financial trade or business.

Sec. 366. Efficient use of currency transaction report system.

Subtitle C--Currency Crimes and Protection

Sec. 371. Bulk cash smuggling into or out of the United States.

Sec. 372. Forfeiture in currency reporting cases.

Sec. 373. Illegal money transmitting businesses.

Sec. 374. Counterfeiting domestic currency and obligations.

Sec. 375. Counterfeiting foreign currency and obligations.

SEC. 2. CONSTRUCTION; SEVERABILITY.

Any provision of this Act held to be invalid or unenforceable by its terms, or as applied to any person or circumstance, shall be construed so as to give it the maximum effect permitted by law, unless such holding shall be one of utter invalidity or unenforceability, in which event such provision shall be deemed severable from this Act and shall not affect the remainder thereof or the application of such provision to other persons not similarly situated or to other, dissimilar circumstances.

TITLE I--ENHANCING DOMESTIC SECURITY AGAINST TERRORISM

SEC. 101. COUNTERTERRORISM FUND.

(a) ESTABLISHMENT; AVAILABILITY- There is hereby established in the Treasury of the United States a separate fund to be known as the `Counter terrorism Fund', amounts in which shall remain available without fiscal year limitation--

(1) to reimburse any Department of Justice component for any costs incurred in connection with--

(A) reestablishing the operational capability of an office or facility that has been damaged or destroyed as the result of any domestic or international terrorism incident;

(B) providing support to counter, investigate, or prosecute domestic or international terrorism, including, without limitation, paying rewards in connection with these activities; and

(C) conducting terrorism threat assessments of Federal agencies and their facilities; and

(2) to reimburse any department or agency of the Federal Government for any costs incurred in connection with detaining in foreign countries individuals accused of acts of terrorism that violate the laws of the United States.

(b) NO EFFECT ON PRIOR APPROPRIATIONS- Subsection (a) shall not be construed to affect the amount or availability of any appropriation to the Counter terrorism Fund made before the date of the enactment of this Act.

SEC. 102. SENSE OF CONGRESS CONDEMNING DISCRIMINATION AGAINST ARAB AND MUSLIM AMERICANS.

(a) FINDINGS- Congress makes the following findings:

(1) Arab Americans, Muslim Americans, and Americans from South Asia play a vital role in our Nation and are entitled to nothing less than the full rights of every American.

(2) The acts of violence that have been taken against Arab and Muslim Americans since the September 11, 2001, attacks against the United States should be and are condemned by all Americans who value freedom.

(3) The concept of individual responsibility for wrongdoing is sacrosanct in American society, and applies equally to all religious, racial, and ethnic groups.

(4) When American citizens commit acts of violence against those who are, or are perceived to be, of Arab or Muslim descent, they should be punished to the full extent of the law.

(5) Muslim Americans have become so fearful of harassment that many Muslim women are changing the way they dress to avoid becoming targets.

(6) Many Arab Americans and Muslim Americans have acted heroically during the attacks on the United States, including Mohammed Salman Hamdani, a 23-year-old New Yorker of Pakistani descent, who is believed to have gone to the World Trade Center to offer rescue assistance and is now missing.

(b) SENSE OF CONGRESS- It is the sense of Congress that--

(1) the civil rights and civil liberties of all Americans, including Arab Americans, Muslim Americans, and Americans from South Asia, must be protected, and that every effort must be taken to preserve their safety;

(2) any acts of violence or discrimination against any Americans be condemned; and

(3) the Nation is called upon to recognize the patriotism of fellow citizens from all ethnic, racial, and religious backgrounds.

SEC. 103. INCREASED FUNDING FOR THE TECHNICAL SUPPORT CENTER AT THE FEDERAL BUREAU OF INVESTIGATION.

There are authorized to be appropriated for the Technical Support Center established in section 811 of the Antiterrorism and Effective Death Penalty Act of 1996 (Public Law 104-132) to help meet the demands for activities to combat terrorism and support and enhance the technical support and tactical operations of the FBI, $200,000,000 for each of the fiscal years 2002, 2003, and 2004.

SEC. 104. REQUESTS FOR MILITARY ASSISTANCE TO ENFORCE PROHIBITION IN CERTAIN EMERGENCIES.

Section 2332e of title 18, United States Code, is amended--

(1) by striking `2332c' and inserting `2332a'; and

(2) by striking `chemical'.

SEC. 105. EXPANSION OF NATIONAL ELECTRONIC CRIME TASK FORCE INITIATIVE.

The Director of the United States Secret Service shall take appropriate actions to develop a national network of electronic crime task forces, based on the New York Electronic Crimes Task Force model, throughout the United States, for the purpose of preventing, detecting, and investigating various forms of electronic crimes, including potential terrorist attacks against critical infrastructure and financial payment systems.

SEC. 106. PRESIDENTIAL AUTHORITY.

Section 203 of the International Emergency Powers Act (50 C. 1702) is amended--

(1) in subsection (a)(1)--

(A) at the end of subparagraph (A) (flush to that subparagraph), by striking `; and' and inserting a comma and the following:

`by any person, or with respect to any property, subject to the jurisdiction of the United States;';

(B) in subparagraph (B)--

(i) by inserting `, block during the pendency of an investigation' after `investigate'; and

(ii) by striking `interest;' and inserting `interest by any person, or with respect to any property, subject to the jurisdiction of the United States; and';

(C) by striking `by any person, or with respect to any property, subject to the jurisdiction of the United States`; and

(D) by inserting at the end the following:

`(C) when the United States is engaged in armed hostilities or has been attacked by a foreign country or foreign nationals, confiscate any property, subject to the jurisdiction of the United States, of any foreign person, foreign organization, or foreign country that he determines has planned, authorized, aided, or engaged in such hostilities or attacks against the United States; and all right, title, and interest in any property so confiscated shall vest, when, as, and upon the terms directed by the President, in such agency or person as the President may designate from time to time, and upon such terms and conditions as the President may prescribe, such interest or property shall be held, used, administered, liquidated, sold, or otherwise dealt with in the interest of and for the benefit of the United States, and such designated agency or person may perform any and all acts incident to the accomplishment or furtherance of these purposes.'; and

(2) by inserting at the end the following:

`(c) CLASSIFIED INFORMATION- In any judicial review of a determination made under this section, if the determination was based on classified information (as defined in section 1(a) of the Classified Information Procedures Act) such information may be submitted to the reviewing court ex parte and in camera. This subsection does not confer or imply any right to judicial review.'.

TITLE II--ENHANCED SURVEILLANCE PROCEDURES

SEC. 201. AUTHORITY TO INTERCEPT WIRE, ORAL, AND ELECTRONIC COMMUNICATIONS RELATING TO TERRORISM.

Section 2516(1) of title 18, United States Code, is amended--

(1) by redesignating paragraph (p), as so redesignated by section 434(2) of the Antiterrorism and Effective Death Penalty Act of 1996 (Public Law 104-132; 110 Stat. 1274), as paragraph (r); and

(2) by inserting after paragraph (p), as so redesignated by section 201(3) of the Illegal Immigration Reform and Immigrant Responsibility Act of 1996 (division C of Public Law 104-208; 110 Stat. 3009-565), the following new paragraph:

`(q) any criminal violation of section 229 (relating to chemical weapons); or sections 2332, 2332a, 2332b, 2332d, 2339A, or 2339B of this title (relating to terrorism); or'.

SEC. 202. AUTHORITY TO INTERCEPT WIRE, ORAL, AND ELECTRONIC COMMUNICATIONS RELATING TO COMPUTER FRAUD AND ABUSE OFFENSES.

Section 2516(1)(c) of title 18, United States Code, is amended by striking `and section 1341 (relating to mail fraud),' and inserting `section 1341 (relating to mail fraud), a felony violation of section 1030 (relating to computer fraud and abuse),'.

SEC. 203. AUTHORITY TO SHARE CRIMINAL INVESTIGATIVE INFORMATION.

(a) AUTHORITY TO SHARE GRAND JURY INFORMATION-

(1) IN GENERAL- Rule 6(e)(3)(C) of the Federal Rules of Criminal Procedure is amended to read as follows:

`(C)(i) Disclosure otherwise prohibited by this rule of matters occurring before the grand jury may also be made--

`(I) when so directed by a court preliminarily to or in connection with a judicial proceeding;

`(II) when permitted by a court at the request of the defendant, upon a showing that grounds may exist for a motion to dismiss the indictment because of matters occurring before the grand jury;

`(III) when the disclosure is made by an attorney for the government to another Federal grand jury;

`(IV) when permitted by a court at the request of an attorney for the government, upon a showing that such matters may disclose a violation of state criminal law, to an appropriate official of a state or subdivision of a state for the purpose of enforcing such law; or

`(V) when the matters involve foreign intelligence or counterintelligence (as defined in section 3 of the National Security Act of 1947 (50 C. 401a)), or foreign intelligence information (as defined in clause (iv) of this subparagraph), to any Federal law enforcement, intelligence, protective, immigration, national defense, or national security official in order to assist the official receiving that information in the performance of his official duties.

`(ii) If the court orders disclosure of matters occurring before the grand jury, the disclosure shall be made in such manner, at such time, and under such conditions as the court may direct.

`(iii) Any Federal official to whom information is disclosed pursuant to clause (i)(V) of this subparagraph may use that information only as necessary in the conduct of that person's official duties subject to any limitations on the unauthorized disclosure of such information. Within a reasonable time after such disclosure, an attorney for the government shall file under seal a notice with the court stating the fact that such information was disclosed and the departments, agencies, or entities to which the disclosure was made.

`(iv) In clause (i)(V) of this subparagraph, the term `foreign intelligence information' means--

`(I) information, whether or not concerning a United States person, that relates to the ability of the United States to protect against--

`(aa) actual or potential attack or other grave hostile acts of-a foreign power or an agent of a foreign power;

`(bb) sabotage or international terrorism by a foreign power or an agent of a foreign power; or

`(cc) clandestine intelligence activities by an intelligence service or network of a foreign power or by an agent of foreign power; or

`(II) information, whether or not concerning a United States person, with respect to a foreign power or foreign territory that relates to--

`(aa) the national defense or the security of the United States; or

`(bb) the conduct of the foreign affairs of the United States.'.

(2) CONFORMING AMENDMENT- Rule 6(e)(3)(D) of the Federal Rules of Criminal Procedure is amended by striking `(e)(3)(C)(i)' and inserting `(e)(3)(C)(i)(I)'.

(b) AUTHORITY TO SHARE ELECTRONIC, WIRE, AND ORAL INTERCEPTION INFORMATION-

(1) LAW ENFORCEMENT- Section 2517 of title 18, United States Code, is amended by inserting at the end the following:

`(6) Any investigative or law enforcement officer, or attorney for the Government, who by any means authorized by this chapter, has obtained knowledge of the contents of any wire, oral, or electronic communication, or evidence derived therefrom, may disclose such contents to any other Federal law enforcement, intelligence, protective, immigration, national defense, or national security official to the extent that such contents include foreign intelligence or counterintelligence (as defined in section 3 of the National Security Act of 1947 (50 C. 401a)), or foreign intelligence information (as defined in subsection (19) of section 2510 of this title), to assist the official who is to receive that information in the performance of his official duties. Any Federal official who receives information pursuant to this provision may use that information only as necessary in the conduct of that person's official duties subject to any limitations on the unauthorized disclosure of such information.'.

(2) DEFINITION- Section 2510 of title 18, United States Code, is amended by--

(A) in paragraph (17), by striking `and' after the semicolon;

(B) in paragraph (18), by striking the period and inserting `; and'; and

(C) by inserting at the end the following:

`(19) `foreign intelligence information' means--

`(A) information, whether or not concerning a United States person, that relates to the ability of the United States to protect against--

`(i) actual or potential attack or other grave hostile acts of a foreign power or an agent of a foreign power;

`(ii) sabotage or international terrorism by a foreign power or an agent of a foreign power; or `(iii) clandestine intelligence activities by an intelligence service or network of a foreign power or by an agent of a foreign power; or

`(B) information, whether or not concerning a United States person, with respect to a foreign power or foreign territory that relates to--

`(i) the national defense or the security of the United States; or

`(ii) the conduct of the foreign affairs of the United States.'.

(c) PROCEDURES- The Attorney General shall establish procedures for the disclosure of information pursuant to section 2517(6) and Rule 6(e)(3)(C)(i)(V) of the Federal Rules of Criminal Procedure that identifies a United States person, as defined in section 101 of the Foreign Intelligence Surveillance Act of 1978 (50 C. 1801)).

(d) FOREIGN INTELLIGENCE INFORMATION-

(1) IN GENERAL- Notwithstanding any other provision of law, it shall be lawful for foreign intelligence or counterintelligence (as defined in section 3 of the National Security Act of 1947 (50 C. 401a)) or foreign intelligence information obtained as part of a criminal investigation to be disclosed to any Federal law enforcement, intelligence, protective, immigration, national defense, or national security official in order to assist the official receiving that information in the performance of his official duties. Any Federal official who receives information pursuant to this provision may use that information only as necessary in the conduct of that person's official duties subject to any limitations on the unauthorized disclosure of such information.

(2) DEFINITION- In this subsection, the term `foreign intelligence information' means--

(A) information, whether or not concerning a United States person, that relates to the ability of the United States to protect against--

(i) actual or potential attack or other grave hostile acts of a foreign power or an agent of a foreign power;

(ii) sabotage or international terrorism by a foreign power or an agent of a foreign power; or

(iii) clandestine intelligence activities by an intelligence service or network of a foreign power or by an agent of a foreign power; or

(B) information, whether or not concerning a United States person, with respect to a foreign power or foreign territory that relates to--

(i) the national defense or the security of the United States; or

(ii) the conduct of the foreign affairs of the United States.

SEC. 204. CLARIFICATION OF INTELLIGENCE EXCEPTIONS FROM LIMITATIONS ON INTERCEPTION AND DISCLOSURE OF WIRE, ORAL, AND ELECTRONIC COMMUNICATIONS.

Section 2511(2)(f) of title 18, United States Code, is amended--

(1) by striking `this chapter or chapter 121' and inserting `this chapter or chapter 121 or 206 of this title'; and

(2) by striking `wire and oral' and inserting `wire, oral, and electronic'.

SEC. 205. EMPLOYMENT OF TRANSLATORS BY THE FEDERAL BUREAU OF INVESTIGATION.

(a) AUTHORITY- The Director of the Federal Bureau of Investigation is authorized to expedite the employment of personnel as translators to support counterterrorism investigations and operations without regard to applicable Federal personnel requirements and limitations.

(b) SECURITY REQUIREMENTS- The Director of the Federal Bureau of Investigation shall establish such security requirements as are necessary for the personnel employed as translators under subsection (a).

(c) REPORT- The Attorney General shall report to the Committees on the Judiciary of the House of Representatives and the Senate on--

(1) the number of translators employed by the FBI and other components of the Department of Justice;

(2) any legal or practical impediments to using translators employed by other Federal, State, or local agencies, on a full, part-time, or shared basis; and

(3) the needs of the FBI for specific translation services in certain languages, and recommendations for meeting those needs.

SEC. 206. ROVING SURVEILLANCE AUTHORITY UNDER THE FOREIGN INTELLIGENCE SURVEILLANCE ACT OF 1978.

Section 105(c)(2)(B) of the Foreign Intelligence Surveillance Act of 1978 (50 C. 1805(c)(2)(B)) is amended by inserting `, or in circumstances where the Court finds that the actions of the target of the application may have the effect of thwarting the identification of a specified person, such other persons,' after `specified person'.

www.ingramcontent.com/pod-product-compliance
Lightning Source LLC
Chambersburg PA
CBHW070655290526
45790CB00001B/327
* 9 7 8 1 4 8 4 9 4 2 7 8 9 *